EZRA POUND, NATURE AND MYTH

Frontispiece: Ezra Pound on the Rapallo sea-front, late 1920s.
(Courtesy of Mary de Rachewiltz).

EZRA POUND, NATURE AND MYTH

Edited by

William Pratt

AMS Press
New York

Library of Congress Cataloging-in-Publication Data

Ezra Pound, Nature and Myth / Edited by William Pratt
  With a Preface by Hugh Kenner.
    p. cm – (AMS Studies in Modern Literature; no. 23)
    Includes bibliographical references and index.
    ISBN 0-404-61593-7 (alk. paper)
    1. Pound, Ezra, 1885-1972—Criticism and interpretation.
    2. Nature in Literature.   3. Myth in Literature.   I. Pratt,
    William, 1927-.   II. Series.
PS3531.O82 Z62176   2002
811' .52—dc21   2002025572
                                                       CIP

AMS Press, Inc.
Brooklyn Navy Yard, Bldg. 292, Suite 417, 63 Flushing Ave.
Brooklyn, New York 11205
U.S.A.

MANUFACTURED IN THE UNITED STATES OF AMERICA

CONTENTS

ILLUSTRATIONS

Frontispiece: Ezra Pound on the Rapallo sea-front, late 1920s (Courtesy of Mary de Rachewiltz)

Preceding Pound's essay, "European Paideuma": (Courtesy of Massimo Bacigalupo)

Fig. 1: "the gardens of Adonis" (note shocks of wheat below altar)

Fig. 2: "The sea-board shrines to the Madonna delle Grazie are NOT oriental." Post-card of the church of Nostra Signora delle Grazie, near Chiavari.

Fig. 3: "Monte Allegro on the limestone heights above Rapallo."

Fig. 4: "The shrines are filled with votive offerings of ship models and pictures of shipwrecks from which the votators have been saved." Votive picture (1904) in the church of Montallegro.

HUGH KENNER

Preface

Pound's scope, lifelong, was encyclopedic; ''Nature and Myth'' is just one of many possible ways to direct attention, for as William Pratt remarks in his Introduction, there is in Pound's poetry ''a constant passage between mortality and immortality,'' especially evident in today's world, wherein the very existence of the divine is a theme for suspicion. His reason for asserting that the gods would not return was simple: ''They have never left us.'' He wrote me once that he could be quite a good Catholic if only he could be allowed to draw up his own list of saints. Another day, during one of my many visits to the Chestnut Ward at St. Elizabeths, he spoke of how a Bible had been issued to every inmate of the Pisan D.T.C., where, he said, he had read it through for the first time. ''I am probably the only person to have read through the Bible *after* reading Confucius.''

And here we likely have a new insight into perhaps his most famous passage of verse. For in the Old Testament, Proverbs VI:6, we find ''Go to the ant, thou sluggard; consider her ways, and be wise,'' with more about how she prepareth her meat in the summer, and gathereth her food in the harvest; while in Ecclesiastes we are told, ''vanity of vanities, saith the Preacher, vanity of vanities; all is vanity.'' These are just a few pages apart, and Pound likely read them the same day. Hence

> The ant's a centaur in his dragon world.
> Pull down thy vanity, it is not man
> Made courage, or made order, or made grace,
>   Pull down thy vanity, I say pull down.
> Learn of the green world what can be thy place
> In scaled invention or true artistry . . .

Sure enough, a few pages later an actual newborn ant is observed in descent ''from mud on the tent roof to Tellus,'' en route to his underearth forebears exactly as Odysseus made his visit to Hades.

So, page after page, Nature and Myth, Myth and Nature, intertwined inextricably. The label ''nature poetry'' is apt to make us think of Wordsworth, wandering lonely as a cloud and spotting a host of innumerable daffodils. Otherwise, English ''poetry'' has been apt to connote London, city of bedrooms and workrooms. True, American poetry has been less city-bound than British. Eliot, though, had his "half-deserted streets" and rooms within which women come and go before he ever moved to England. But lo, Pound "stood still and was a tree amid the wood" in the very first line of *Personae*, and in that one line we already find Nature and Myth intertwined.

WILLIAM PRATT

Introduction

The Gods have not returned. "They have never left us."
They have not returned.

Canto CXIII

For Pound, the modern dilemma was a consciousness divided, caught between the human and the divine. Though he might exclaim in an early poem "See, they return!" and go on to assert in *Guide to Kulchur* that "the gods exist," he was still forced to admit in the last *Cantos* that "The Gods have not returned," even though he himself continued to believe that "They have never left us." Pound as a poet committed himself early to the view expressed in *The Spirit of Romance* that:

> For our basis in nature we rest on the indisputable and very scientific fact that there are in the "normal course of things" certain times, a certain sort of moment more than another, when a man feels his immortality upon him.[1]

Thus Pound wrote poetry in which there is constant passage between mortality and immortality, since for him there was no more doubt about the existence of gods and goddesses than about heroes and heroines; both were part of a permanent world that reached back to the Greeks and even beyond them to the Egyptians and Sumerians and ancient Chinese. His mind was saturated with poetry and therefore with myth, since the two had always been inseparable in the past and he thought they must remain inseparable in the present and future, great poets being divinely inspired to keep their language fresh and vital, "to resuscitate the dead art/Of poetry, to restore the 'sublime,'/In the old sense" as he put it in *Hugh Selwyn Mauberley*.

The difficulty, for the modern poet, was to maintain the connection between the human and the divine when anything divine was suspect, when the natural world was the domain of scientists rather than poets, and poets were forced into arcane pursuits of truth and meaning in order to preserve a reverence for the creative source of being in nature and man, to go on insisting that "it is not man/made courage, or made order, or made grace," as he wrote so memorably in *Canto LXXXI*. For Pound, throughout his long and prolific career, it was necessary to believe in the reality of both nature and myth in order to write poetry at all.

1

Appropriately, then, "Ezra Pound: Nature and Myth" fits all the essays collected in this book. The title was used for the 15th Ezra Pound International Conference at Rapallo in 1993, and many of the papers were first given there, each paper telling in its own way how Pound was able to translate nature—including history—into myth. In doing so, Pound made liberal use of his sources, whether Chinese or Japanese or Greek or Latin or Anglo-Saxon or Celtic or French or Italian; he also, as this volume amply demonstrates, invented traditions at will. He combined Greek gods and heroes, goddesses and heroines, never hesitating to lump Aphrodite-Venus with Eleanor-Helen or Persephone-Kore or Circe-Cunizza to fashion feminine ideals, nor to link Zeus-Jupiter with Dionysus-Christ-Tammuz or Odysseus-Aeneas-Bertrand de Born as masculine ideals. All of these mythical-historical figures were part of his metamorphic tradition of visionary experience, in which the natural or historical became the mythical and the mythical became the natural or historical.

This metamorphic tradition was inherent in the imagination of Pound. At Rapallo, his chosen place of residence in Italy from 1925 on, Pound worked from the nature surrounding him in the cliffs of the Ligurian Sea directly into myth, bringing Mary-Aphrodite into birth from the bells of the little church of San Pantaleo, high above Rapallo, or Tammuz-Adonis from the sea-lights which were placed in the Gulf of Tigullio every July in honor of the Virgin Mary:

'Tamuz! Tamuz!'

    They set lights now in the sea
        and the sea's claw gathers them outward.
    The peasant wives hide cocoons now
        under their aprons

        for Tamuz   *Canto 91*

Pound had read in Plutarch and used in *Canto 23* the story of Anchises sailing near an island where the cry of Adonis reaches the boat. The cry was the public lamentation for the death of Adonis, who was also called Tamuz. In *Canto 91*, Pound combines the cry that Plutarch recorded and the old Ligurian custom of floating lights in the water, which he could see every July in Rapallo from his balcony overlooking the waterfront, during the festivities for the Madonna of Montallegro (who was believed locally to have appeared there to a peasant on 2 July 1557). Just as Anchises heard the cry in Mycenean times, so Pound in the twentieth century encountered ritual forms which he thought were examples of an ancient beauty periodically recovered and recalled—a beauty connected with fertility and vegetation, as the image of "the peasant wives" hiding "cocoons now under their aprons" suggests. Myth had not disappeared from common life, but was still available to him in the annual ceremonies he observed at Rapallo.

Pound was a Modernist in his understanding of myth, since he made myth more aesthetic than religious (in contrast to Eliot, who made myth more religious than aesthetic). The whole tendency of Pound's work can be called *mythopoeic*, a union of imagination and vision, and he pioneered in exploring a reality that included both nature and myth, a reality limited neither to the purely realistic nor to the purely visionary.

Readers of Pound's poetry have often been intimidated by his scholarship, which was vast, but was—as many of these essays reveal—arbitrary and even contradictory: what mattered most to him was to produce great poetry, by whatever means he might choose. Pound could cavalierly ignore the scholarly virtues of accuracy and consistency if it suited him; on the other hand, he was an amazing virtuoso with language who could practice poetic virtues of imagination never dreamed of by scholars. When Alan Peacock deals in his essay with Pound's use of the Latin poet Catullus as an inspiration for Imagism, he shows how easily Pound's mind moved from ancient to modern, so that if Pound admitted it was beyond his ability to provide an adequate translation of the poetry of Catullus directly into English, he could import the diction and wit of Catullus in Latin into the making of new images in English, giving them the "clarity" and "hardness" he sought.

Though this volume is filled with such impressive scholarly interpretations of Pound, the end of all poetic criticism and scholarship is a better understanding of the poetry, and Pound's poetry offers an ingenious fusion of scholarly interests with the sort of refreshment to the mind which poetry best provides. What is clear from this collection is that Pound's poetry remains fascinating to readers around the world, partly because it presents so many challenges as well as refreshments to the mind, and an international gathering of experts such as this book presents seems peculiarly necessary for understanding Pound's poetry. No wonder such a gathering has occurred many times before and is likely to occur many times again, until the time arrives—if it ever does—when readers of Pound are satisfied that his work has been fully and exhaustively interpreted.

Readers of Pound know that he deliberately chose Rapallo on the Italian Riviera as a place to live, but they may not know that he was constantly inspired in his poetry by the landscape around him in this mountainous, castled seaside resort on the Gulf of Tigullio. Pound made the Rapallo landscape into myth, translating real sights and sounds into mythical equivalents, so that when the sexton of the historic little San Pantaleo church, high above the Rapallo harbor in Sant'Ambrogio, rang out Verdi's aria from *Rigoletto*, "La donna e mobile," ("woman is fickle") on his bells, Pound's mind moved from the Madonna figure of Christians to the Aphrodite figure of the Greeks without hindrance. Pound delighted in transforming natural events or spectacles into myth, especially in moving from the Christian to the pagan as he often did in his poetry. He was particularly taken with the sight of the small votive lights sent out to sea in the annual festival of the Madonna of Montallegro in the Tigullian Gulf every July—"From the long boats they have set lights in the water" as he wrote in *Canto 47*, and echoed with "they set lights now in the sea" in *Canto 91*—because to him it was an old religious ceremony in a Catholic country, dating from a legendary seventeenth century vision of the Virgin Mary by a fisherman, which Pound freely associated with the rebirth of Tammuz in Babylonian myth and the Gardens of Adonis of Greek myth, much more ancient symbols of resurrection.

Pound delighted in being controversial—"One good attack is worth twenty eulogies," he once told me[2]—easily making his own interpretation of the Eleusinian Mysteries (still mysteries to most Greek archeologists and scholars) to sacralize the sexual act in the rites practiced in the Greek temple. Pound was as liberal with Chinese or Japanese history and myth as he was with Greek, making his transformations or metamorphoses the more readily because the Chinese culture—first beautifully translated in the poems of *Cathay*—was more remote from him than the Greek. Pound's ability to move nature and history around in his imagination, to adapt and create myth from his surroundings, is a chief vehicle of his poetry, as all the essays in this book demonstrate in one way or another.

Pound might mythify himself as Odysseus or Dionysus or Sigismondo da Malatesta, or he might mythify his mistress, Olga, as Circe or Aphrodite or Persephone or Cunizza, parallelling the material of his own life mythically, as Anne Conover Carson suggests in her biographical sketch of Olga Rudge as the person nearest to Pound in his later years. The intriguing triangle of Pound and his wife Dorothy and his mistress Olga at Rapallo is portrayed by Carson as alternately trying and amusing, with Pound spending his mornings with his wife in their apartment overlooking the harbor of Rapallo and his afternoons with his mistress in her house at Sant'Ambrogio high above the town. She particularly notes how Olga saw herself as both the woman and the myth, willingly assisting Pound with her music to compose his *Cantos*, casting a spell over him by her violin playing as Circe's sorcery had enchanted Ulysses. At times, Pound would compose his *Cantos* in her presence and she would note the experience in her diary, referring once to Pound's anger as creative, because he remarked to her "how useful a fit of rage was for starting and keeping one at work." Their worst moments were during the Second World War, when all three women—wife, mistress, and daughter—were forced to live cooped up in Olga's house, Pound torn between the two women he loved who were insanely jealous of each other, until the Italian partisans came to arrest him in 1945 and remove him to the detention camp at Pisa where he wrote what many regard as his finest sequence, the *Pisan Cantos*.

There is no question that Pound made myths out of personal history in his poetry, but in another mood, he might derive his Circe/Aphrodite figure from history, in the person of Eleanor of Aquitaine (analogous to the mythical Helen of Troy), as Philip Grover suggests in his treatment of Pound and the French troubadours, or from a figure as remote as the Hagoromo nymph of Japanese Noh drama, as Peter Makin attests in another essay. Pound could equate Western with Eastern culture, and often did so, but more often he used what he called the "European Paideuma," as in the Dionysus/Bacchus/Iacchus/Zagreus of Greek myth, which Massimo Pesaresi traces in his study of the various names which Pound uses for the Greek god. Michael Faherty shows in his paper that Pound also made use of Celtic myth, equating the old Irish division between the "corporal" and "aetherial" self with the division between the human and divine, and evoking in his early poems and again in his late *Pisan Cantos* the madness of King Goll, which Yeats had derived from the Madness of Sweeney in Irish legend, both being figures who like Peire Vidal the French troubadour or like Pound at Pisa were disgraced and condemned to wander mad and to sleep outdoors exposed to the elements.

Even where Pound is most "natural," as Richard Caddel acknowledges in his essay on Modernist Ecology, his work still has its recognizable mythical aspect, since the individuality of his principle, "oak leaf not plane leaf," implies a sovereign purpose at work in nature, though unlike earlier "nature poets" such as Wordsworth or John Clare, Pound looked at nature with both a scientist's and a mythmaker's eyes, seeing the miracle of a baby wasp emerging from its mother's mudcase at Pisa as if he were witnessing the Eleusinian mysteries of death and rebirth, the soul entering the earth in death and emerging again alive. Caddel represents one approach of Pound to nature where he is most scientific, most like Agassiz or Fabre, the scientific naturalists he admired, and most unlike Wordsworth the Romantic nature poet, while Peter Nicholls shows Pound as the Modern nature poet who freely interwove time and history with nature, using the Noh drama as a model for his imagination to work with in recovering and revitalizing the past in the present.

All of these essays show the variety of Poundian observation and vision, stretching the mind of the reader to follow the poet in his odyssey through space and time, which may lead downward to the darkness of Hell as well as upward to the brightness of Heaven, just as Dante's journey led in his *Divine Comedy*, Pound's chief model for *The Cantos*. My essay on "Pound's Hells, Real and Imaginary," is intended to show that Pound compares with the greatest epic poets of Western literature—Homer, Vergil, Dante, or Milton—in his willingness to "descend into the world of the dead," as he put it, through his imagination, whether using Sextus Propertius or Ulysses as his guide, but in his later years being forced to suffer the real hell on earth of his imprisonment at Pisa and later at St. Elizabeths. Pound works both imaginary and real hells into his poetry, especially in *The Cantos*.

Most of these essays do deal with *The Cantos*, that lifework which took fifty years to complete and was left still unfinished at the end, because it is Pound's endless epic which presents the most challenges to his readers, "a poem containing history" as he defined it, but also containing much besides history—autobiography and literary allusion and natural observation. No single reader can do justice to Pound's *Cantos*, nor to his work as a whole, and that is why an Ezra Pound International Conference has been held nineteen times since 1976 when Philip Grover convened the first one at Sheffield, and why the sixteenth Ezra Pound International Conference was convened once more by Philip Grover in 1995 in Brantôme, in Perigord, at the center of the France of the Provencal troubadours—the medieval Provence which was for Pound a mythical landscape as well as a historical one, the troubadour Bertrand de Born in his castle at Hautefort serving as Pound's historical alter ego, while the lady Maent was his mythical—even if she was not his historical—mistress. Since Brantôme, Pound conferences have been held at his daughter's castle of Brunnenburg in 1997, in Beijing, China, in 1999, and at the Sorbonne in Paris in 2001; the twentieth Ezra Pound International Conference will be held in his birthplace of Hailey, Idaho, and nearby Sun Valley in 2003.

Pound held the view that myths come from human responses to nature (and to what is beyond nature, "the gods" or nymphs or whatever invisible beings exist in the universe), not from reading the rationalizations of mythographers or historical scholars of literature. So Peter Makin could argue plausibly enough in his paper that the nymph Hagoromo of Japanese Noh drama, remote though she is to Western readers, may bear some resemblance to Venus and Cunizza and the swan-maidens of Western myths, or that at least such a resemblance is suggested in Pound's poetry, and Peter Nicholls could go on to argue in his paper that the whole Japanese tradition of Noh drama provided Pound with a unity of image in a longer literary form, thus easing his transition from the short Imagist poem to the longer *Cantos*. Pound's use of nature and myth in his poetry combined both the miraculous and the real, the ancient and the modern, and these essays should help to increase the recognition that Ezra Pound, the American expatriate born on the Western frontier in Hailey, Idaho, who chose to live much of his life in the seaside resort of Rapallo on the Italian Riviera, created a body of world poetry that compares with the best in any language or time, providing eloquent testimony to the enduring legacy he left behind.

Pound's own essay, "European Paideuma," with which this collection begins, was written a year after his *Guide to Kulchur*, but it is a much shorter essay setting forth his idea of world culture. He called it "European Paideuma," because he wanted to adopt the Classical Greek synonym for "culture" which the German anthropologist and folklorist Leo Frobenius favored, and which Pound came to prefer. Indeed, in his *Guide to Kulchur* in 1938, he gave full credit for the attribution, saying "Frobenius uses the term Paideuma for the tangle or complex of the inrooted ideas of any period."[3] Pound's essay is consistent therefore with his thinking at that time, but it was really composed in the form of a letter, written to an American scholar working at Frobenius' Forschungsinstitut für Kulturmorphologie in Germany.[4] Though it was quoted in part in Charles Norman's biography of *Ezra Pound* (1960), it has never been published in its entirety in a book until now.

The essay appears here because it bears directly on the topic of *Ezra Pound, Nature and Myth*. In it, Pound, in his typically allusive and telegraphic style, argued that reality and belief are always connected, and that poetry embeds in words the fundamental connection between what is visible and what remains invisible, which he described in a famous passage of the *Pisan Cantos* as a process of gradual enlightenment: "First came the seen, then thus the palpable/ Elysium, though it were in the halls of Hell." (*Canto LXXXI*) To Pound, seeing was literally believing: he espoused Imagism early in his career as a way of raising physical sight into metaphysical vision, and later he adopted the Chinese ideogram, or picture-writing, as a method of generating poetry through a complex of perceptions, a superposition of verbal images. When, still later, he made *Kulchur* or *Paideuma* his broadest aim in *The Cantos*, he was simply lifting his sight once again, from the level of space to the level of time and history, trying to encompass in his poetry observation as well as knowledge, seeing as well as reflection, nature as well as myth.

"European Paideuma" stemmed immediately from the *Guide to Kulchur* written in Rapallo, which Pound mentions, but it also came from a much earlier work he also mentions, written in London and published serially in *The New Age* in 1911–12, under the mystifying title of "I Gather the Limbs of Osiris." His title referred to the Egyptian cult of Isis, which held that the goddess Isis resuscitated her dead brother, Osiris, after he was dismembered by an evil brother named Set. Osiris became the Judge of the Dead for the Egyptians, and Pound with his capacity for taking in all the world's myths pictured himself as one who could, like Isis, restore life to the dead. He tried in his writing to revive all legitimate beliefs, and especially, as he would later say in *Hugh Selwyn Mauberley*, "to resuscitate the dead art/ of poetry, to restore 'the sublime'/in the old sense." His early series of essays had expounded at length his theory, which he had first put forth in *The Spirit of Romance* in 1910, that art "remains the permanent basis of psychology and metaphysics," that in other words art embodies knowledge of human nature which science has not superseded.

So Pound's lifelong fascination with world poetry had led him early in his career to voice a belief that accuracy of language always came from accuracy of observation, and that masterpieces were written by those rare individuals who were able to perceive the cosmos inside themselves, and express it not only for themselves but for others, since "We are nevertheless one humanity, compounded of one mud and of one aether."[5] For Pound, nature (mud) and myth (aether) were mixed in man, who as an artist sought to show at once what was tangible and what was intangible in human experience. If he succeeded in becoming a great artist, then his technique was equal to his inspiration, and Pound admired above all others the artists whose techniques were the test and measure of their sincerity, Homer and Dante supremely. To the youthful Pound, to "gather the limbs of Osiris" was what the true artist does in every age: he resurrects the living from the dead by the truthfulness and exactness of his expression.

Thus, we may view "European Paideuma" as another statement, by an older Pound, of his perennial theory of artistic Renaissance: the rediscovery of old masterpieces leads to the creation of new masterpieces. The European Renaissance (itself an expression of the European Paideuma) had taken place in the Late Middle Ages, when in his view first the Italians, then the French, and then the English had rediscovered the Classical Greeks, whose masterworks of visual and verbal arts inspired new works of painting, sculpture, poetry. As the Greeks worked from nature into myth, and the Renaissance artists followed their example, so, Pound fervently believed, artists could do once more in his own time. Pound was never troubled by whether the myths were originally pagan or Christian; in fact, he preferred to mix the pagan and the Christian in his own poetry, as he saw the women of Rapallo do when they brought their lighted boats or "gardens of Adonis" to the Gulf of Tigullio in the July festival for the Virgin Mary: as they, in his view, united Aphrodite and Mary in their vision of heaven, so Pound sought to bring these two goddesses together in his own poetry. Whether by resurrecting dead artists like Homer or Dante, or dead gods like Osiris or Dionysus or Christ, Pound believed that art could bring the living back from the dead, and in his own poetry he sought to fuse nature with myth, taking a Chinese poet like Li Po (Rihaku of *Cathay*) or the Japanese Noh plays as his models as easily as he might take Greek or Latin or Anglo-Saxon poets as models. Pound's "European Paideuma" was in fact not limited to European artists or gods, for in his *Cantos* he was as capable of appropriating the African rain-gods of Leo Frobenius' researches, "Frobenius der Geheimrat der im Baluba das Gewitter gemacht hat" ("Frobenius the Counselor drummed up a storm in Africa," as Pound says in *Canto LXXIV*), as he was of appropriating Sumerian hieroglyphics ("A man's paradise is his own nature" Pound states in *Canto XCIII*); in his essay, he even speaks of a Nordic Confucius as an authentic possibility.

Pound's imagination was as polyvalent as the mind of Ulysses, taking in every language and every culture to form its overarching *Paideuma*, and although at the time he wrote his essay he was directing it to a German audience from Italy (not omitting the anti-Semitism which was the dark underside of his Fascism), he showed there, as elsewhere in his prose and poetry, that he credited Classical Roman order along with Medieval French courts of love, Arab mathematicians along with Italians of the Quattrocento (the high Renaissance of the Fifteenth Century), because all helped to form what he liked to call the ''European Paideuma.''

In fact, Pound's short essay is even more inclusive than his longer *Guide to Kulchur*, and it is consistent in its world-embracing outlook, despite the marks it shows of the time when it was written, which was the eve of the Second World War, the world-shaking conflict which brought him to his knees, ''As a lone ant from a broken anthill/From the wreckage of Europe, ego scriptor,'' he would later put it in *Canto LXXVI*. When Pound says in his essay that ''The Madonna of the Italian peasant is to my knowledge a LOCAL divinity,'' he is speaking from long experience of living in Rapallo, where the Christian ceremonies were imbued with popular significance. And when he ends with the pronouncement that ''the European nature is to act, observe, and believe,'' he is attesting to an attitude that made Pound himself as an American poet a European—which may have led him to expatriate himself to England, France, and Italy from 1908 until his arrest in 1944, and then to return to Italy, from exile as a traitor to his native country, after his release from St. Elizabeths in 1958, and to live there until his death in Venice in 1972. Pound's ''European Paideuma'' was in fact a world culture fashioned by his own mind, expounded in his prose and embodied in his poetry, all in all the most complete synthesis attempted by any writer or artist in the entire Twentieth Century. His essay of 1939 then, brief though it is and hastily composed, limited in some ways by its time and place, is nevertheless an expression of the many-sidedness of Pound's genius, the true subject of this book, which all the essays here included are meant to cover.

NOTES

1. Ezra Pound, *The Spirit of Romance* (1910, reprinted New York: New Directions, n.d.),4.

2. William Pratt, "The Greatest Poet in Captivity: Ezra Pound at St. Elizabeths," *Sewanee Review* (Autumn, 1986), 625.

3. Ezra Pound, *Guide to Kulchur* (New York: New Directions, [1938]), p. 57.}

4. Their collaboration is evidenced in the book about prehistoric African rock-painting they produced before Pound wrote his letter: see Leo Frobenius and Douglas C. Fox, *African Genesis* (New York: Benjamin Blom, 1937).

5. "I Gather the Limbs of Osiris," in William Cookson, Ed., *Ezra Pound: Selected Prose, 1909–1965* (London: Faber & Faber, 1973), 32–33.

Fig. 1. ''The gardens of Adonis'' (note shocks of wheat below altar)

Fig. 2. "The sea-board shrines to the Madonna delle Grazie are NOT oriental." Post-card of the church of Nostra Signora delle Grazie, near Chiavari.

Fig. 3. "Monte Allegro on the limestone heights above Rapallo."

Fig. 4. "The shrines are filled with votive offerings of ship models and pictures of shipwrecks from which the votators have been saved." Votive picture (1904) in the church of Montallegro.

1

EZRA POUND

European Paideuma[1]

(1939)

Edited with an Afterword
by Massimo Bacigalupo

To hell with Spengler. What we believe is EUROPEAN. In this essay I distinguish between "intelligence" and "intellect" using the latter term to indicate the mental scaffolding men erect to deal with what they don't understand. Belief is from intelligence.

From the crying "Ligo" in Lithuania (to a sun freed of its winter imprisonment),[2] down to the Greek archipelago, certain things are believed. Book instruction obscures them. The people in Rapallo rushing down into the sea on Easter morning or bringing their gardens of Adonis [Plate I] to church on the Thursday before, have not learned it in school.[3] Neither have the peasant women read anything telling them about bringing silk-cocoons to church carefully concealed in their hands or under their aprons.[4]

The Xtian Church was of very mixed elements. The valid elements European. The Church went out of business about A.D. 1500, semitized from two forces, one usury, and the other the revival of Jewish texts (Old Testament). The only vigorous feasts of the Church are grafted onto European roots, the sun, the grain, the harvest and Aphrodite.

The folklorists have woefully neglected Ovid, a very serious compiler of known feasts.

The Church went out of business when belief ceased. When, from fear, they condemned the long buried Scotus Erigena who had said "authority comes from right reason" and had defined sin as "a lapse from reality."

The amour courtois, the hidden intentions of the Ghibelline poets, are by no means negligible. Some students, L. Valli for example, have intellectualized too far, have tried to interpret too much, and from an inadequate understanding, also from an unwillingness to leave the unknown as just that, to admit that there is a great deal NOT recorded and to which they have no key.[5] The code of the amour courtois, the love doctrine, is found in the Georgian "Man in the Panther Skin."[6] The valid, as distinct from the invalid Arabian elements need not and certainly should not before deep examination be grouped among non-European roots.

11

What the Arabs carried from Greece, is ours, and need not be credited to the Semite. It is a pity, for the sake of our mental grasp, that the curious researchers have so often been led off onto Buddhism; onto corpse worship and ghost worship, and flopped into theosophy rather than sticking to a search for belief.

The for the present extremely unfashionable Swinburne had, I think, at one time belief ("Ballad of Life" and "Julian Apostate").[7]

He also knew more Greek than any Englishman after the happy days of Porson[8] and Savage Landor.

In the teeth of current snobbisms I have pointed out that the German pavillion at last year's Venetian biennial exposition was the best pavillion.[9] The visitor with any kind of unperverted form sense should have seen this. The failure to understand the new turn in the arts is due partly to dulness, but even more to stultification by art-merchants propaganda (which has gone on with steady infection for at least 50 years).

I am not here trying to prove anything, I am asking for a direction of effort and research onto the sorting out of sound and unsound elements.

Greek sculptors made gods, Romans, emperors, Italians of the Quattrocento individuals; but all in a proper direction. Leonardo wanted to know true proportions, so did Petrus de Burgo before him.[10]

The function of Germany, as I see it, in the next forty years' art is indispensable. Nowhere else is there enough force toward a purgation. The Italians are too easy going. Spain is African and Christian, and you can not trust Christianity for ten minutes, it is full of Semitic microbes. They have been implanted in its terminology, the overflowing of Roman order, of Roman concept, graduation and hierarchy by Oriental terminology has left too septic a verbal mass for any unwary reader or hearer to trust himself loose in.

There are bits of Egypt in the fans used in high ceremony, phallic mitres put on and removed—mixed into all there is too much contagious allusion. The religious element is to a great extent Pagan, but mere Paganism is not enough. The intellectual elements are admittedly Plato and Aristotle, the latter largely destructive of faith, of belief in the sense I have used the word in my opening paragraph.

Sound ethic we have from Confucius via Mencius. Their disciples were horrified by the immorality and anti-social nature of Christianity and for a long time kept it out of China on those grounds. The tradition[al] portrait of Confucius shows him a Nordic. There is no more reason to doubt the authenticity of the portrait than to doubt the stone heads of the Caesars. Chinese ethics from the 40th parallel; Athens 38th; Rome 42nd.

The whole of romance, mediaeval legend, Venusberg, Tristan is ineradicably OF belief. As are feasts of planting and harvest and feasts of the turn of the sun. Say Aphrodite, Adonis, Helios.

We need a much more careful analysis of the Dionysus cult before we decide what parts of it are valid.

It is ridiculous to say that Europe is naturally without religion. That statement has been used tendentiously by the pandifiers,[11] by the schizophrenics and by those who from questionable motives have wished to weaken all Europe. All this Malthusianism, corpse-worship, anti-fecundity, ghost-worship is suspect (or considerably more than) fecal analysis, anal psychology.

One may, and many good men have wished to do honor to the intellectual (vide definition in my opening paragraph) structure built up by the Roman Church from the time of St. Ambrose down to the Renaissance. Let us affirm again that the valid parts of this thought are Roman, with possibly a touch of the Hellenic.

Botticelli is indubitably European, 100% European. The Quattrocento is the most European century in our record. We must reinspect Leo Frobenius' graphs. How far South of the 38th parallel can we go without great alertness and unsleeping suspicion of every belief, every idea, every ceremonial gesture or every form-characteristic.

We can NOT permit short nobbly curves. It is measure vs/bigotry and fanaticism. Not for nothing is one of our reviews called Gerarchia, hierarchy.[12] Along with Frobenius' study I offer my notes on "Mediaevalism" in my Cavalcanti and my "Ethics of Mencius" (Criterion, July 1938).

I should like to see my *Guide to Kulchur* in a German translation, however chopped and allusive, and to a systematic mind, I suppose, very unsatisfactory, that little volume may prove. Fighting on several fronts, and of necessity extremely unpopular with a press controlled by usurers and a book trade swamped by the press, I have not an unlimited supply of printer's time at my disposal. I have to get down the essentials when some publisher has the rashness to charter me. The live thinker must put in the mortar and connecting bits for himself.

I want, badly, German correspondents and answers. I want suggestions and additions. I am aware of the fragmentary state of my own knowledge. But I had, at least, the grace to entitle a series of notes back in 1910 "I Gather the Limbs of Osiris."

In the struggle to present or boot-leg the results of Frobenius' life work into America and Western Europe I think it would be useful for someone in the Forschungsinstitut to gather into a 200–page volume (Roman type) a brief list of the distinctly EUROPEAN beliefs encountered in the total mass of Frobenius' writings. Better, of course, if there could be an English translation.

That would be one book. Another volume could be usefully composed in analysis of the falsification and distortion of European belief. Vulcan into Thor, or not. Vulcan provided with a tail and made part of a Semitic mythology, or not.

In all this one should not slight the European factors of Christianity. The sea-board shrines to the Madonna delle Grazie [Plate II] are NOT oriental.[13] These have most emphatically NOT come from Palestine. There is no need of going "hay-wire" and seeing pink mice. The Madonna of the Italian peasant is to my knowledge a LOCAL (raumlich) divinity. It is their Madonna, present in a given ambience.

We need a wholly new and far more rigorous examination of the records of the Bacchic invasion. The toys of Bacchus were found in feast at Auxerre, I think the feast of Corpus, but it may have been Holy Week.[14] But this is not enough for us to go on. There is that ambiguous borderline along the 38th parallel. At the date of the Dionysic invasion there is no reason to suppose the cult itself wasn't already a melange.[15]

Again I assert that there is one disease which one can stigmatize as utterly unEuropean. The European does NOT get hold of an idiotic text, proclaim it infallible or authoritative and then proceed to explain it, to give it meanings extraneous to its verbal formulation, and worship it. This plague and infection is from the Near East.

As I understand it the European nature is to act, observe and believe. (In this order of processes.)

An attempt to superimpose a nonsensical verbal formulation on his good sense brings the sort of comment that John Hargrave[16] has made on T.S. Eliot's Anglo-Catholicism: "lots of dead cod about a dead god." Hargrave being I think at least as religious a man as Mr. Eliot. Instead of calling the European non-religious one would do better to say that he backs his instinct against an obviously tricky or foolish text. Searching for truth he sees no reason to ham-string himself with a formula which may or may not have been constructed in the course of honest search for a difficult verity.

MASSIMO BACIGALUPO

Afterword

Ezra Pound wrote "European Paideuma" in 1939 when, having just returned from the U.S., he was sorting out elements to be used in the later *Cantos*, and thinking about the respective merits of Western and Eastern religions. This makes it particularly interesting for readers of his poetry, it being possibly his only full statement on religion in English after *Guide to Kulchur*. (He was to return to the subject, in Italian, in the *Meridiano di Roma* articles and especially in "Carta da visita.")[17]

Pound sent "European Paideuma" on 7 August 1939 to Douglas C. Fox at the Forschungsinstitut für Kulturmorphologie in Frankfurt, asking if he could see to its publication "anywhere in Germany where it will get serious attention/ better translated into German I think." Fox, according to Charles Norman who interviewed him for his biography of Pound and quoted from Pound's letters to him, was "a young and personable American, Frobenius's assistant," and had spent time with Pound and James Laughlin at the Salzburg Festival in summer, 1935. Fox told Norman that since Pound often wrote to Frankfurt for information on anthropological subjects and nobody could decipher his letters, "I, as the only American there, was made special correspondent for Pound. Sometimes I did not get what E.P. was driving at either . . . But, we communicated, and Pound apparently got the feeling that here was someone who understood. I was not so certain".[18] So "European Paideuma" was sent off as part of a letter to Fox with the barest introductory remarks about Fox seeing to its translation.

Fox replied promptly on 9 August 1939, agreeing to translate the article and submit it to the prestigious *Frankfurter Allgemeine Zeitung*. He said that he had already written to the editor of *Germany and You* a propaganda journal published in English suggesting that he print the English version. Fox was losing no time. He was the kind of correspondent that Pound got only too rarely—a knowledgeable person who was curious and friendly enough to try to find out what Pound was thinking, without either dismissing his statements offhand or taking them as unquestionable verities. So what was already an unusually attractive piece of writing by Pound, treating of the kind of material he wanted for his poetry, found an unusually attentive reader. In his courteous response, Fox risked Pound's wrath by querying a number of typically obscure and portentous allusions in the original draft, and asking him to expand them for the benefit of German readers:

FORSCHUNGSINSTITUT FÜR KULTURMORPHOLOGIE
Frankfurt A.M., den 9.8.39
Stiftstrasse 30

Dear Mr. Pound:

Thank you for your letter. I'll translate it and try to get it into the Frankfurter Zeitung, which is the best paper published in this country. If I have no luck I'll do my best to dispose of it elsewhere. Have written the editor of Germany and You for suggestions and have also suggested that he publish the English version. If not, we can send that end of it to Duncan.

As you know, the Germans are sticklers for thoroughness and they like to know details—particularly if said details "humanize" a given subject. I'm too ignorant to fill them in and so I'm going to trouble you with a lot of questions.

1. What is the crying "Ligo" and why does it yowl?

2. Adonis, I gather, is also a flower. Is it brought to church as an offering? to have the seeds blessed? to promote fertility? as a testament to beauty? etc.

3. Cocoons. Damned interesting. Do the women bring them every Sunday or any Sunday? What is behind it (apparently)? Is the system widespread? Where?

4. I had thought Scotus was a writer, not a work. Is the S. Erigena one of his works? Date? (circa) (Sorry to ask dam questions, but it cannot be helped.)

5. "Some students as L. Valli, for example, have intellectualized too far etc." A quotation from Valli or one of the others illustrating how they intellectualized too far would help.

6. For Nazis and myself not properly acquainted with the amour courtois of Provence the "Man in the Panther Skin" needs amplification.

7. "Valid as distinct from invalid Arabian elements." Examples of both.

8. "What the Arabs carried from Greece" Mathematics?

9. Names of researchers who have turned to Buddhism, corpse worship, etc.

10. Quote from Swinburne illustrating belief.

11. Why was the German pavillion in Venice the best?

12. "The intellectual elements are admittedly Plato and Aristotle etc." One or two sentences of amplification.

13. "The whole of romance etc. is of belief" A bit of amplification.

14. "Feasts of planting and harvest etc." This I can amplify if you care to have me do so.

15. Madonna delle Grazie. Very good. Short description of the peasants' attitude to the Madonna would make it still better.

16. What are the records of the Bacchic invasion? Archaeological and literary? Would it be possible to give sources, to say in what way they were examined and in what way they should be examined? "Date of the dionysic invasion" (circa?) Are not Dionysus and Bacchus two very different conceptions?

17. One more paragraph needed for conclusion. "The European believes that" etc., or "bases his belief on" etc. A positive note in closing. What the European does not do has been very well said. Now a strong word about what he does and will do should round the thing off properly. Or so it seems to me.

I hope you will have patience with my questions. It is clear that you will probably have to thumb your notes a bit to answer some of them—and that means work. But the article, which I like very much, will be all the better for it. And the more scholarly an interpretation is—provided it has the life which is inseparable from your work—the easier it is (in this country) to get it printed. I'm looking forward to translating it and hope to be able to do it justice.

When you have the time I'd like to hear some of your impressions of America and how it goes with Cummings, Laughlin, Iris Barry and others. Please give my regards to Mrs. Pound.

With all good wishes,

Sincerely yours,

Douglas C. Fox.[19]

Pound obliged at least in part and sent Fox a few additional lines for a conclusion, in which however he characteristically insisted again on what the European does *not* do, this time choosing the worship of texts (such as the Bible) as something negative and peculiarly non-European. In this he was picking up his old complaints about mindless philology and the cult of laundry lists, besides attempting to define once again the Biblical or Jewish "plague and infection." Pound's protest against the canonization and worship of a text is interesting in the light of recent readings of the Jewish tradition as "text-centered." On the other hand, there is a dramatic irony in Pound's statement, for it could be shown that *The Cantos* are based precisely on a sort of worship of texts, regardless of their "verbal formulation"—for Pound is always quoting his authorities which are supposed to carry conviction just by being named. Furthermore, *The Cantos* are addressed to readers who are ready to take them as a kind of sacred text, and not to look too closely at their inconsistencies and half-truths. What matters is that they are song (canto), word, text, ideograph.

Pound kept a carbon of this additional passage, but apparently not of the accompanying message, in which he answered a few of Fox's questions. This important letter has not come to light. However, Fox prepared an edited version of "European Paideuma," adding some footnotes and bits of information provided by Pound. These refer to Fox's queries 1, 2, 3, 4, 5, 10, 15, 17. Pound seems to have kept silent about the interesting question 6, the answer to which many of his readers would have liked to know, for it would have cast light on a central but tantalizing reference in *Cantos 48* and *74* (*digenes*, later *digonos*). I have incorporated the additional information in the version of "European Paideuma" printed here, with the exception of the amplification of the reference to Erigena. Fox's version reads: "For it must have been fear that prompted it [the Church], in 1208, a century or so after the man's death, to exhume the bones of Scotus Erigenia [sic] and to damn him as an unbeliever. Scotus' crime had been his intelligence. For he had said," etc. Some of the wording is doubtless Pound's, but his readers will be unlikely to misunderstand "the long buried Scotus Erigena" as a work rather than a writer, as Fox did.

On the whole, Fox's edited version is less successful than Pound's original draft. Fox tried to bring some logic to the argument, rearranged the paragraphs, omitted or toned down racy and objectionable passages, and provided a more cautious and scholarly veneer, thereby losing the liveliness which, as he well saw, was the essence of Pound's appeal. The edited version is only of interest for what it tells us of the extra information that Fox was able to elicit from Pound. Both versions remained unpublished. Hitler invaded Poland a few weeks after they were written, and Fox returned to New York, thus ceasing to function as Pound's intended contact with Germany. Pound reminded him of the article in a subsequent letter to the U.S.:

> Whether the F/Zeitung now wants yr/ translation of my remarks on European Paideuma I don't know.
>   I keep chewing on that. Wheat god. In fact now that I have about finished with economics mebbe some sucker will putt up something for a less COMprehensible subject, namely religion taken sul serio, not Mr. Eliot's pale Galilean rubbish.[20]

But clearly no commission was forthcoming at such at a time for Pound's revisitation of Swinburnian paganism. Later he must have lost interest in "European Paideuma," written as it was for a German audience at a very particular time.

Yet Pound's notes and his additional explanations relating to Adonis, the cocoons of the Zoagli silk-weavers, and the Madonna delle Grazie, as included in the version presented here, are exciting for all readers of *The Cantos*, for they are very much at the center of that poem's idea of the numinous and of its "sagetrieb"[21]—the respect for vegetal powers, with its unpleasant Wagnerian codicil condemning the "butchers of lesser cattle," and the worship of the motherly and compassionate goddess of all seafarers: the "venerandam" of *Canto 1*, and the "EUPLOIA" of *Canto 106*, associated with seashells and nautiluses as in *Canto 80*, reappearing elsewhere in the guise of Leucothea or Isis Kuanon. From Cyprus to Montallegro to Zephyrium to Torcello—Pound's Ulysses has worshipped her in many shrines across the Mediterranean, and beyond. "At Miwo the moon's axe is renewed. . . . "[22] Pound the Rapallo anthropologist and the worshipper in the little churches like San Pantaleo and the Madonna delle Grazie (near Chiavari) is perhaps the more likable of the poet's many personae. And *The Cantos* are a periplus but also a prayer, an address to the Lady: "M'elevasti," "compassion."[23] They are also a sort of ex voto, and could easily be placed near the naive pictures of happy rescues in one of those seaboard shrines.[24]

NOTES

1. This essay was sent as part of a letter of 7 August 1939 to Douglas Fox, Forschungsinstitut für Kulturmorphologie, Frankfurt, with the following introductory remarks: "Dear Fox, As you may know, I have been in America, etc/ . . . Is there anywhere in Germany you can usefully print the following, where it will get serious attention. Better translated into German, I think." This indicates that Pound was addressing a German audience, with particular reference to the anthropological interests of the Institute founded by Leo Frobenius for which Fox, an American, worked. (Frobenius, who had died in 1938, had developed the concept of "paideuma," a word which Pound uses roughly as a practical and unsolemn equivalent of "culture.") After querying Pound on various points, Fox prepared an edited and toned-down version of the essay (subsequently referred to as F), as he had done with an earlier Pound article, "Totalitarian Scholarship and the New Paideuma," *Germany and You.* 25 April 1937 (Gallup C 1405). The present text is that of Pound's original draft, never before published in its entirety. A few phrases and notes are added from F, see footnotes. Capitalization and punctuation have been regularized, and obvious typing errors have been corrected. The Fox-Pound correspondence relating to "European Paideuma" is in the Collection of American Literature, Beinecke Rare Book and Manuscript Library, Yale University, to the staff of which I have been much indebted over the years. I hereby acknowledge permission to cite copyright material as follows: Unpublished works by Ezra Pound: Copyright @ 2001 by Mary de Rachewiltz and Omar S. Pound. Used by permission of New Directions Publishing Corporation.

2. The parenthetical phrase is added in F. Fox had asked Pound: "What is the crying 'Ligo', and why does it yowl?" My friend Adolfas Mekas reports hearing a similar cry in Latvia in 1949, and quotes as follows from his diary: "For the Latvians last night was a great holiday—as pagan as the search for the fern blossom that brings luck. They wore on their heads wreaths made of leaves, and sang all night—liguo! liguo! They chanted that word for hours, the whole night." (25 June 1949)

3. "Shoots prematurely forced. The seeds are put on wet flannel, sprout early and are a part of the Easter decoration in the Rapallo churches."—Pound's note, added in F as a result of Fox's queries. For details on these "gardens of Adonis," known in Italy as "sepolcri" because they symbolize the Holy Sepulchre, see Massimo Bacigalupo, "Pound's Tigullio," *Paideuma* 14,

2–3 (1985), p. 188, and Plate 15, p. 205. For the custom of running to the sea mentioned by Pound see Tomaso Rabajoli, "Tradizioni della Settimana Santa sulla costa e nell'entroterra," *Il Golfo* (Chiavari) 9 (April 1987), pp. 25–26: "A ritual passed down from one generation to another at the sound of the 'Gloria' on the morning of Easter Saturday, was to run to the nearest fountain or to the seashore to wash one's face . . . to gather the onda nuova (new wave)."

4. "This custom is not a matter of common knowledge even in Rapallo." —Pound's note, added in F as a result of Fox's queries. Actually, the women did not bring the cocoons to church but the eggs of silkworms. Pound refers to this tradition in *Cantos 85* and *91*.

5. Pound discusses at length Luigi Valli's *Il linguaggio segreto di Dante e dei Fedeli d'Amore* (1928, rpt. Milan: Luni Editrice, 1994), in "Cavalcanti" (reprinted in *Literary Essays*) and *Guide to Kulchur*. Valli published a second volume in 1930, in which he replied to his critics. He died in 1931. Both volumes are reprinted in the 1994 edition, see review in *Il Sole-24 Ore*, 11 December 1994, p. 25.

6. See Shota Rustaveli, *The Man in the Panther Skin: A Romantic Epic*, trans. Marjory Scott Waldrop (London: Oriental Translation Fund, 1912). Fox asked Pound to explain the allusion, but apparently got no answer, and the reference is dropped in F. Pound cites Rustaveli's twelfth-century epic also in the title (but not in the text) of the 1942 article, "Nella pelle di pantera" (Gallup C1642) and in a letter to his son-in-law Boris de Rachewiltz from Washington, D.C., June 18, 1954, Pound asked: "Is The man in the panther skin translated from Georgian into Italian? [in margin: Georgian epos connected Provencal Troubadour Anschauung] There is an English translation. Whether it was in 'The Quest', G. R. S. Mead's quarterly, I dont know" (Berg Collection, New York Public Library). "The Quest" ran in 1912 two articles on Georgian myths by J. Javakhishvili, but no translation of *The Man in the Panther Skin*, which Pound certainly read in the 1912 edition. According to Basilius Sadathierashvili, Rustaveli's national epic "recalls the erotic genre of Ariosto and Ovid, while its ethical-philosophical ideas take us back to a certain kind of Neo-Platonism, and its mysticism and metaphysics point to Oriental philosophical conceptions, yet it has an unmistakeable individuality—the fusion of the Eastern and Western element, typical of Georgian culture, finds in the poem its greatest and most homogeneous expression"—*Dizionario letterario Bompiani delle opere e dei personaggi di tutti i tempi e di tutte le letterature* (Milan: Bompiani, 1950), II, 185.

7. References in parentheses added in F. Fox had asked for "Quotes from Swinburne illustrating belief."

8. Richard Porson (1759–1808), English classical scholar.

9. The Venice Biennale has been held biennially (with interruptions) since its inauguration in 1895. Most countries have an independent pavillion. Pound often was in Venice for part of the summer, when the Biennale is on view. The 1938 Biennale ran from 1 June-30 September. The German selection featured only the kind of works that had official approval: academic portrayals of landscapes, peasants, cows, athletes, and busts of Hitler and Mussolini. On the other hand, the Italian pavillion included works by reputable artists like Felice Casorati, Carlo Carra, Giacomo Manzu. See illustrations in catalogue, "XXI Esposizione Biennale Internazionale d'Arte." Pound's unaccountable praise for the German selection shows how far he had come from his Vorticist days with his new "totalitarian" poetics.

10. A reference to Piero della Francesca, born c. 1416 in Borgo San Sepolcro, who also wrote technical treatises such as De prospectiva pingendi. Pound mentions him in *Canto 8* ("maestro di pintore"), *Canto 45* ("Pier della Francesca") and *Guide to Kulchur*, ch. 23 ("Pietro di Borgo").

11. "Paudifiers" is the word in Pound's text. F reads "pacifiers," which doesn't fit the context.

12. Official Fascist periodical (Milan, 1922–43), formerly edited by Benito Mussolini.

13. "Sailor shrines at points commanding a view of the sea, for instance that on Monte Allegro on the limestone heights above Rapallo. [See Plate 3] The shrines are filled with votive offerings of ship models and pictures of shipwrecks from which the votators have been saved. [Plate 4] 'Hang me bells in Venus' shrine.' "—Pound's note, added in F as a result of Fox's queries. For Pound's use of this motif in his poetry see "Draft of *Canto 75*," *Paideuma*, 20, 1–2 (1991), p. 37, and *Canto 106*. For reproductions of pictures or "ex votos" now in Montallegro, see *Ex voto a Montallegro* (Rapallo: Comune, 1989), and Massimo Bacigalupo, "Pound's Tigullio," Plate 13, p. 204. The sanctuary of the Madonna delle Grazie is on the road descending from Zoagli to Chiavari. The Pounds must have hiked there often, for there is a drawing of the church in Dorothy's book, *Etruscan Gate: A Notebook with Drawings and Watercolours*, ed. Moelwyn Merchant (Exeter: Rougemont Press, 1971).

14. See *Canto 77* ("the dancing at Corpus the toys in the/service at Auxerre").

15. The essay in its original form ends here, followed by a "Private Postcript" as follows: "Dear D2C.F. I think you told me Klages was not serious character??? However, I shd. like to look into that. I shd/ like for some Eng/ or U.S. mag/ a note of german neo-pagans, and attempts to be greek or whatever. even if it is mere back wash of Walter Pater/ the more likely to be backstillfurtherwash of Goethe's papa. One damn trouble is that the researchers go hindoo/ of all the damned/ or theosophic/ which is NO bloody use. none of these highfalutin pretenses to know the beyond is any good. parlor paganism/ to be guarded against as are parlor pinks. phrase might be used. yrz E." Ludwig Klages (1872–1956), also mentioned in Canto 75, was the author of *Mensch und Erde* (1933) and other works of spiritual philosophy viewed favorably by the Nazis. In his response of 9 August Fox asked Pound to provide "one more paragraph . . . for conclusion." Pound obliged with the sentences that are here added to the original essay.

16. John Gordon Hargrave (1894–1982), exponent of Social Credit, leader of the Green Shirts of England.

17. See also "Statues of Gods" (Gallup C1515), "On the Degrees of Honesty in Various Occidental religions" (C1520), "Religio" (C1523). The first of these articles (published in *Townsman* for August 1939, the same month in which "European Paideuma" was written) is in fact a compact version of "European Paideuma," and reverts to the Rapallo rituals.

18. Charles Norman, *Ezra Pound*, rev. ed. (New York: Minerva Press, 1969), pp. 374.

19. An abridged version of F appears in *Ezra Pound, Machine Art and Other Writings: The Lost Thought of the Italian Years*, ed. Maria Luisa Ardizzone (Durham: Duke Univ. Press, 1996), pp. 131–34. Some paragraphs from the original draft are quoted in Norman, *Ezra Pound*, pp. 3–73.

20. Quoted by Norman, *Ezra Pound*, p. 374. No date given. Probably late 1939. "Sul serio" is Italian for "seriously." "Pale Galilean" is a quotation from A. C. Swinburne, "Hymn to Proserpine," line 35.

21. Pound's word for "the oral tradition," see *Cantos 85* and *90*. The "butchers of lesser cattle" mentioned in the next line are berated in *Canto 93*. Pound favors hunters and agriculturalists as against nomad shepherds.

22. *Canto 106*—alluding to the Noh play *Hagoromo*.

23. Quoted from two passages of invocation, *Cantos 90* and *93*.

24. See above, footnote 13.

2

ANNE CONOVER CARSON

Her Name Was Courage: Olga Rudge, Pound's Muse and the "Circe/Aphrodite" of the Cantos

> That her acts
>   Olga's acts
>   of beauty
>   be remembered.
>
> Her name was Courage
> & is written Olga
>
> These lines are for the
>   ultimate CANTO
>
> Whatever I may write
>   in the interim.

Ezra Pound, Cantos (Fragment 1966)

The woman who had the last word in the *Cantos* and in Ezra Pound's personal life was Olga Rudge, the concert violinist, his companion of some 49 years and mother of his only daughter, Mary. Olga endured during the best of times and the worst of times, and after the poet's death, was the keeper of the flame.

Her name was indeed "courage" as caretaker of the poet in his later years. She described her position in a letter to a friend: "Looking after EP is a full-time *job*! [her emphasis] . . . a 'heavy' role . . . [I am] a blessing and a damned nuisance!—sec[retary], cook & bottle washer . . . counter-irritant & soporific, all in one bottle—and sometimes I feel as if the bottle had been given a good shaking before taking!"[1]

Olga's lifelong commitment to the poet may be viewed as worth her sacrifice, when we consider that although Pound began to publish the *Cantos* in 1917, after their meeting he incorporated the persona of "the trim-coiffed goddess" into his earlier work, and Olga was the muse who inspired him in finishing his epic.

Pound often sent manuscripts to Olga to read and to comment on. As early as 1925, he wrote: "Speaking of collections, IF she has any STRONG

ideas as to which poems he shd. and shd. NOT put in his collected edtn. she
SPEAK.''[2] Again, ''He has, he thinks, cleared up that line in vii, the Canto that
she said was obscure. Has she any more suggestions while he is getting ready
for a noo edtn?''[3]

It would be impossible in this paper to cite all of the allusions to Olga
Rudge in the *Cantos*, or all of the passages relating to Olga's life with the poet.
The emphasis in this brief overview will be on the most important themes and
places, gleaned from several years of research, especially among the Olga Rudge
Papers at the Beinecke Library, Yale University, some 15 feet of shelf-space
containing the daily (sometimes twice daily) correspondence between two highly
intelligent and articulate people that sheds new light on the *Cantos*. Olga—who
early believed in Pound's genius—collected and saved every scrap of paper,
from the first blue *pneumatique* messages (in Paris in the 1920s) until the end
of Pound's life in 1972. She continued to record her memories, thoughts and
activities in a daily journal into her nineties. In writing the first biography of
this extraordinary woman, I have also drawn upon the personal memorabilia of
Olga Rudge at Brunnenburg, the archives of the Accademia Musicale Chigiana
in Siena and many other archival resources, as well as personal interviews
with her daughter Mary de Rachewiltz, her friends and colleagues, and Olga
Rudge herself.

In an article for the *New Age* magazine, Pound wrote:

> ''[America] has produced what is to my mind a very interesting
> type of woman . . . a woman of broad experience, of compre-
> hension, usually of generous humour, a woman whose acquain-
> tance with life has been first hand and various . . . [she] may
> be said to have some sort of human experience unconditioned
> by sex or caste.''[4]

He might well have been describing the Ohio-born Olga Rudge, although at the
time that was written, they had not yet met. They were to meet some years later
at a salon in Natalie Barney's mansion with mock-Greek Temple à l'Amitié in
Paris. Recalling the occasion, Olga wrote to Pound at St. Elizabeths in 1961:
''Does He know that Natalie's friends are thinking of a tribute for her 85th
birthday? I suppose it wouldn't be proper for Her to say, 'I thank you,' Natalie,
for Him! (I mean introducing Him, 20 rue Jacob).''[5] In *Canto 80*, Pound refers
to *The old trees near the rue Jacob* and to Barney: *Natalie said to the apache:
vous êtes très mal élevé* (p.519).

Also in *Canto 80*, Pound describes the apartment on the Rue Washington
that Judith Gautier inherited from her father, the great poet Théophile: *Judith's
junk shop with Théophile's armchair* (p.518), which Olga had visited as a child
with her mother, the concert singer Julia O'Connell. In the 1920s when Pound

was a guest in the Gautier flat, it was tenanted by the avant-garde translator and occultist, Mademoiselle Claire de Pratz, yet still furnished with various bibelots (Chinese, Hindu, and prehistoric) collected by Théophile and passed on to his daughter. In an interview many years later, Olga said that she doubted that Pound would have noticed her if she had not been wearing the Chinese jacket; she caught his eye because of his interest in Confucius and the poetry of Li T'ao Po he was then translating with the aid of Ernest Fenollosa's notes.[6]

At that time, Olga was still living in her late mother's flat near the Gautier place, on the Rue Chamfort bordering the Bois de Boulogne in the choice 16th Arrondissement. "Mother always insisted that we live in beautiful places," Olga said in an interview. And they did. To further her own career as a concert singer, Julia early removed Olga and her two brothers from the unsophisticated steel town of Youngstown, Ohio, first to New York, then to London, and finally Paris, where Olga studied with the renowned first violinist of the Opera Comique, Leon Carambat. She often played for Julia's guests before graduating to the concert stage at nineteen.

In 1923, when Pound first met Olga, he was composing an opera, *Testament de Villon*, and promoting the careers of young musical talents as a critic writing under the pen name "William Atheling." In reviewing one of Olga's early concerts in London, Pound wrote in *New Age* magazine that he "was charmed by the delicate firmness of her fiddling."[7] After they met, he arranged a concert with George Antheil, the avant-garde composer and pianist (first mentioned in *Canto 74*, p.441), who said of Olga: "I discovered when we commenced playing a Mozart sonata . . . [she] was a consummate violinist. I have heard . . . none with the superb lower register of the D and G strings that was Olga's exclusively."[8] In 1926, Olga performed the violin solo in *Testament de Villon* at the Salle Pleyel, and later, several incidental pieces, *Sujet pour violin* and *Fiddle Music, First Suite* which Pound composed especially for her. (Throughout the *Cantos* there are musical themes, as in *Canto 82*, where Pound compares the birds perched on the wire at the Pisan compound to musical notes on a staff: *write the birds in their treble scale/ Terreus! Terreus! . . . / Three solemn half-notes; with their white downy chests black-rimmed/ on the middle wire* [pp.539, 541]). Their mutual interest in music was one of the many bonds that held the poet and muse together.

In *Patria Mia*, Pound limned his pantheon of women: Ceres, the mother type; Juno, the British matron ("propriety and social position to be maintained, no-one's comfort to be considered . . . women of this type have been always, and thank God, always will be, deceived by their husbands"[!]); Pallas Athene, the much-pitied intellectual (in Canto 79, Pound would add, "cd/ have done with more sex appeal"); and Aphrodite—*enough said!*"[EP's emphasis].[9]

We have only to examine the early *Cantos* to discover Olga's place in the pantheon as that of the Aphrodite figure or Circe the "witch goddess," particularly associated with sexual regeneration and union with Odysseus/ Pound. In Pound's theory of sexual function and creativity, the role of woman was to be the passive receptacle for man's sperm, a secondary role in the creative process, but an essential one, nonetheless.[10] But not just any woman would serve as the receptacle for the poet's creative upspurts. Only with an artistic and accomplished woman would Pound consider forming a permanent liaison.

In early photos, Olga appears as a striking young woman, her hair "bobbed" and parted in the middle in the fashion of the Twenties, *simplex munditis* [plain in her neatness] *as the hair of Circe* (*Canto 80*, p.508). Her periwinkle blue or violet eyes are first mentioned by Pound in *Canto 74*, p.460: *her eyes as in "La Nascita"* (the Birth of Venus by Botticelli), and again in *Cantos 96 and 97*: *with eyes pervanche,/ all under the Moon is under Fortuna* (p.670); *Even Aquinas could not demote her, Fortuna,/ violet, pervanche, deep iris,* (p.692). Olga served not only as a model in the writing of the *Cantos*, but as the positive force that assisted in the creative process, the wind at the poet's back, not the negative force that turned Odysseus's men into swine. Her role is also closely linked to that of the Muses, the sister goddesses who presided over song and poetry.

Canto I sets the stage, when Pound/Odysseus first "slept in Circe's ingle." The sexually-charged interpretation of the spell cast by Circe over Odysseus and his men is the core of the Odyssey and of the *Cantos*. Throughout, the poet returns to the theme of Circe/Aphrodite as a positive life force, the "cunni cultrix," as she administers Molu to Odysseus to free him from the evil spell cast over his men.

One of the first clear references to Olga and her world is the central episode of *Canto 23*, where Pound/Odysseus stands with a companion at a window on a hill overlooking the sea, watching men on the beach below emptying sand from their boats (p.108). Looking back on their years together, Olga wrote in 1975: "The terraces of olive trees above the Via Aurelia, between Rapallo and Zoagli overlooking the Gulf of Tigullio . . . were a corner of the Ligurian landscape we both loved. Pound knew it first in 1923, and made it 'Canto country.' The house known locally as 'la casa del poeta' [is now on] a road branching from the Via Aurelia and encircling San Pantaleo and Sant' Ambrogio, which has opened up access to magnificent vistas, . . . until ten years ago, the reward of climbing the steep 'salitas' or mule paths."[11]

In 1929, Olga first came to live for part of the year in the second storey of Casa 60, Sant'Ambrogio, a contadino's house above the salita. *Canto 39* opens "when I lay in the ingle of Circe" (Olga's house), with an olive press on the ground floor (p.193); the *thkk thgk* sound of the press suggested to the poet the clacking of Circe's loom, and Olga practicing her violin evoked "Circe singing with sweet voice, as she went to and fro."[12]

·

Her presence there inspired Pound to organize a series of concerts and to dream of the seaside resort as a center of a "new culture." His interest in music, which began in London and Paris, became increasingly important during the Rapallo years when he worked closely with Olga in promoting the works of modern composers and in rediscovering the "lost" works of the seventeenth century Venetian composer, Antonio Vivaldi. Desmond Chute, the British priest who lived in Rapallo, testifies that those were paradisal years for Pound: "He was seeking his 'island,' on the Riviera di Levante, by the 'green clear and blue clear Tyrrhenian Sea,' "[13] and he found it.

In some respects, one can say that those were less than idyllic years for Olga. The hills above Rapallo were a different world from the ambience of her mother's apartment in Paris, where Olga stopped over between concerts in the cultural capitals of Europe. No indoor plumbing, no electricity, only candlelight. Stella Bowen wrote that every room was surrounded with windows (with an incredible view of the sea), and although Olga had "almost no material possessions, her well-proportioned rooms furnished with big rectangles of sunshine had a monastic air . . . highly conducive to the making of music."[14] In a 1931 diary, Olga recorded: " . . . [We had] macaroni for dinner [cooked] on a spirit lamp, & E. opened a tin of preserved fruit . . . [I] played before dinner, Mozart Concerto #4, Brahms A min. sonata, Schumann for contrast (which did *not* please), and the Beethoven Kruetzer. After, He asked to be allowed to play on my 2nd best fiddle with worst bow, & played with unexpected delicacy and none of [the] roughness one might expect. Whenever *I* play, He never just listens & leaves it at that, it always sets Him off, composing or wanting to play himself."[15]

In the early *Cantos*, Pound describes nature in its many moods in Sant'Ambrogio and nearby Zoagli, for example, *Canto 46*: *that day there was cloud over Zoagli/ . . . and for three days, snow cloud over the sea,* (p.231); and, in one of the most beautiful passages (*Canto 47*): *they have set lights in the water,/ The sea's claw gathers them outward . . . /in the pale night the small lamps float seaward,* (p. 236), referring to the votive lights set adrift in the Gulf of Tigullio on the night of July 3 in homage to the Virgin, while the "sea's claw" (i.e., the mountain wind) gathers them up and pushes them away from the land.

In *Canto 51*—to cite another example of nature and Olga's influence on the Cantos—the poet refers to two of the most popular patterns in flycasting; the first eight lines instruct how to make a fly and suggest the best and only times to use it. *Blue dun; number 2 in most rivers/ for dark days, when it is cold/ A starling's wing will give you the colour/ or duck widgeon, if you take feather from under the wing/ Let the body be of blue fox fur, or a water rat's/ or grey squirrel's. Take this with a portion of mohair/ and a cock's hackle for legs./ 12th of March to 2nd of April.* Pound's source was a book on flycasting written by Olga's Irish grandfather, James O'Connell of Limerick, from which we discovered notes for the *Cantos* in Pound's own handwriting. In a 1975 journal, Olga recorded a robbery at Casa 60, from which thieves took (among other objects of purely sentimental value) "skeins of pure yellow silk, my grandfather's—a great fisherman. In the only known portrait, in his fishing book, he is shown holding some of [the skeins] which, as a child, I learnt were used in making a fly to catch fish with."[16]

In *Canto 91*: *The water-bugs' mittens/ petal the rock beneath,/ the natrix glides sapphire into the rock pool* (p.630), as the poet observes the reflections in the water below Sant'Ambrogio at sunset. In a letter to Katue Kitasono, he asks: "I wonder if it is clear that I mean the shadows of the 'mittens'? and can you ideograph it; very like petals of blossoms."[17] Again, in *Canto 114*, Pound watches the *sea, blue under cliffs* and remembers *William* [W.B. Yeats] *murmuring "Sligo in heaven" when the mist came/ to Tigullio* [p.807].

These were very productive years for Pound, and we have a glimpse of the creative process of the poet in Olga's 1931 diary: "E. came at 4 o'clock, nervous & unsettled, only stayed an hour, then rushed down hill, giving me [an] appt. at Castello [for dinner] at 8, where he turned up with a new Canto. So now I know why he has been having kittens. He says it is not yet sewed together. He corrected at table." Several days later, she wrote: "E. went on typing with awful explosions of swearing & singing—then threw me over the Adams canto [34] upon which new canto celebrated in fitting manner . . . [When] things were not going right, it was told me 'to observe how useful a fit of rage was for starting and keeping one at work.' "[18]

In *Cantos 74–84*, the Pisan landscape serves as a backdrop for the 60–year-old poet's reminiscences: . . . *eucalyptus that is for memory/ under the olives, by cypress, mare Tirreno* (p.449); . . . *bathers like small birds under hawk's eye/ shrank back under the cliff's edge at Il Pozzetto* (*Canto 74*, p.452), referring to the small crescent beach where Pound and Olga bathed in the Gulf of Tigullio. The poet's thoughts return to . . . *our craggy cliffs/ . . . by la vecchia sotto S. Pantaleone/ . . . From il triedro to the Castellaro/ the olives grey over grey holding walls* (*Canto 76*, p.466), where he walked with his daughter to the place the three roads meet: "in the setting sun . . . along the hill path to the old Roman road, above the new Aurelia by the sea . . . past the church to the very edge of the hill where one looks down on the cliffs of Zoagli." There, he *lay on soft grass by the cliff's edge/ with the sea 30 metres below . . . /clear over bed rock* (p.471), watching *the flying azure of the wing'd fish under Zoagli* (p.473).

Mary wrote that when she and her father approached Casa 60 from the *salita*, they could hear Olga practicing: "Mamile had placed the iron music stand in the center of the room, and herself in front of the window[19]: . . . *as against half light . . . /with the sea beyond making horizon le contre-jour the line of the cameo/ profile "to carve Achaia" a dream passing over the face in half-light/ Venere, Cytherea . . . "beauty is difficult"* (*Canto 74*, p.458).

In *Canto 76*, Olga becomes ''Eurus as comforter'' [the southwest wind], *benecomata dea* [the fair-haired goddess], and Aphrodite, linked with Thetis and Maya. For the first time, the poet in his Pisan prison confesses his love for La Cara (Olga): *O white-chested martin, god damn it,/ as no-one else will carry a message, say to la Cara; amo* [p.473].

Pound's painful domestic situation is alluded to in *Canto 78*, the days and nights divided between Dorothy, his wife in Rapallo, and Olga, on the hill above. (One can imagine Olga's pain when she looked down over the cliffs of Zoagli on a clear day; she could almost pick out the familiar figures on the promenade in front of the Pounds' apartment.) Surely this must have been on the poet's mind when he wrote: *No hay amor sin celos/ Sin secreto no hay amor* [There is no love without jealousy; without secrecy there is no love.]

Pound's divided loyalty was put to the test during World War II when Olga's Venice house was sequestered as alien property, and the Pounds' oceanfront flat in Rapallo was taken over by occupying German troops in May 1944. Ezra and Dorothy took refuge up the hill with Olga in Sant'Ambrogio for the duration. ''Baccin,'' who said *I planted that/ tree (Canto 87*, p. 587), refers to the old peasant, G. Solari, who helped to carry ''the accumulation of twenty years of books, papers, letters, manuscripts and drawings'' from the Via Salaria up the hill. Olga left a note for Pound saying, ''Baccin will be at the steps back of the station at foot of *salita cerisola* at quarter to ten domani lunedi. He can wait there as he has the wall to rest load on . . . [I] will be back in time for lunch.'' In a 1945 diary, Olga noted that there were German bunkers on ''the beach below casa 60 [where] E. & I go down afternoons and bathe. I take down tea and we have it *alone* on the beach.''[20] Again, in *Canto 87, . . . bombs fell, but not quite on Sant'Ambrogio/* (p.587) evokes the time when the heavy bombing of the Ligurian coast by the Allies miraculously missed Casa 60.

AOI!/ a leaf in the current (Canto 81, p. 533) best expresses Olga's feelings during that era, though to many observers, the two ladies and one gentleman appeared to coexist in harmony. Mary wrote: ''Never have I seen Mamile cry so unrestrainedly as when she read *Canto 81*: the cry AOI! is an outburst more personal than any other in the *Cantos* and expresses the stress of almost two years when [Pound] was pent up with two women who loved him, whom he loved, and who coldly hated each other.''[21] The cry, AOI! was borrowed from the Japanese Noh play, *Kinuta*, in which the long-suffering wife dies from grief when her husband departs for the capital and stays for three years without sending a message. It perhaps expresses the poet's attempt to understand the feelings of *both* women. In Mary's words, ''I had a glimpse of the madness and the vision: Zeus-Hera-Dione, the two different consorts of one god, one a sky goddess and one an earth goddess . . . Many shades of emotion remain hidden, embedded in the Cantos as mythology.''[23]

At Pisa, the poet remembered the day in May 1945 when the difficult menage-à-trois ended and the partisans knocked abruptly on the door of Casa 60 to take him into custody. He left with a slim volume of Confucius in his pocket and *one eucalyptus pip/ from the salita that goes up from Rapallo* (*Canto 80*, p.514). Olga, who was not there at the time, soon followed downhill to Zoagli, then to U.S. Army headquarters in Lavagna, from which they were both taken by jeep to the Counter Intelligence Center in Genoa. Olga spent several anxious days with Ezra while the military decided what to do with him. When she returned, Dorothy was gone.

Transferred to the Detention Training Center near Pisa, Pound composed some of his finest poetry. Olga wrote to the poet in his prison, "As long as you can go on spinning yourself a cocoon of Cantos, I shall not worry about you."[23]

In *Canto 90*, the descriptions of Castalia were based on Pound's memory of the Sant'Ambrogio coastline: *Castalia is the name of the fount in the hills fold/ the sea below/ narrow beach/*; *Castalia like the moonlight/ and the waves rise and fall/*; *And to Castalia/ water jets from the rock* (pp.619–21). The poet had never visited Delphi at the time these lines were written, but in their last years together, Olga arranged a trip to Greece (1965) so that the poet might see the place where the water nymph pursued by Apollo leapt into the spring that bears her name.

Beginning in the Fifth Decad of the Middle Cantos, the scene shifts to Siena, another site of major importance to Olga and the composition of the *Cantos*. In the realm of Duke Leopold of Tuscany and the founding fathers of the Monte dei Paschi Bank, Pound relies heavily on his knowledge of Sienese history, but Olga's presence is felt; the poet visited her there many times. In July 1936, she wrote to Pound a list of items to bring on his next visit, "Vivaldi ms. [and] photos I had done in Turin," and said that he would find her at Via Roma 22 (2nd floor), the Palazzini Senesi, with a brass plaque on the door. In a letter to Olga from St. Elizabeths, Pound mentioned his "nostalgia di Siena—oni that's no KOREKT word for it,"[24] and Olga replied: "Would she like to be back in Capoquadri or on [the] terrazzo of [the] little flat near [the] market or at [the] end of [the] garden in [the] via Roma flat, where she never could get Him to *sit*."[25] In *Guide to Kulchur*, Pound mentions "a few evenings in the Palazzo Capoquadri listening to Mozart's music," undoubtedly accompanied by Olga.[26]

In the 1930s and '40s, Olga acted as administrative secretary to Count Guido Chigi Saracini, Fondatore and Presidente of the Accademia Musicale Chigiana, a courtly patron of the arts, whose ancestors had fulfilled the same function since the Renaissance (as mentioned by Pound in *Canto 42*, p.214). Olga described "His Nibs," Count Chigi having his portrait painted in a "truly magnificent uniform of the Knights of Malta, red sash, blue-black coat, with large white 'X' on shoulder."[27]

In *Canto 74*, Pound gives a glimpse of Olga as she appeared at a dinner party at the Chigi palazzo: *. . . she did her hair in small ringlets, a la 1880 it might have been/ red, and the dress she wore Drecol or Lanvin/ a great goddess* (p. 449). The count was charmed by Olga; he noticed she had chosen to wear the Chigi family's heraldic red. Under Olga's administration, the Accademia was credited with initiating the great Vivaldi revival, having rescued the long-forgotten manuscripts of the baroque composer from the National Library in Turin. Olga felt a special affinity for the "Red Priest" with the Titian hair because Vivaldi composed for his own—and Olga's—instrument, the violin. In a 1943 letter, the count teased her about "her passionate and inalterable love for that noted priest, bit of a scamp that he was . . . as great an artist as he was undeniably a womanizer and an impenitent satyr . . . given the mores of the times, the *Prete Rosso's* blood must be flowing in your veins."[28]

But for Olga, there was only one great love in her life. She wrote to Pound: "Have discovered some very good walks outside Siena —out one way & back another, so when He comes . . . He bring some feet He can walk in."[29] Mary, visiting her parents, recalled that her father "showed me Siena, stone by stone; . . . the Monte dei Paschi and . . . the various doors and fountains of the town . . . the frescoes of Simone Martini [in the Sala del Mappamondo] . . . - where *Riccio on his horse rides still to Montepulciano*. His favorite walk was to Fontebranda and . . . San Domenico . . . or out into the country towards the convent of Osservanza that stood out . . . serene above the olives."[30] (In *Canto 80*, the poet would recall *the Osservanza . . . broken, and the best de la Robbia busted to flinders* by the bombs of war [p.5ll]).

Looking back on those years from the detention center at Pisa, the poet also remembered *the kallipygous Sienese females* climbing the steep streets, the grass springing from the roof of San Giorgio . . . *weed sprout over cornice*, the preparation for the Palio: *four fat oxen/ having their arses wiped/ and in general being tidied up/ . . . with stoles of Imperial purple/ with tassels, and grooms before the carroccio/ on which carroch six lion heads/ to receive the wax offering* (*Canto 43*, p.216). Again, *Torre! Torre! Civetta! . . . and the parade, and the carrocchio and the flag play/ and the tossing of the flags of the contrade* (*Canto 78*, p.510) referring to the medieval pageant and horse race reenacted every August in the Piazza del Campo, which we know from letters that Pound attended with Olga. In 1937, copying his unmistakable style, she wrote to Pound: "Well she wuz eggspected in the Palazzo where she now is in green brocade suite . . . She has a contrada [costume] for him, but they are very ugly."[31]

With Olga, Pound also attended a concert of modern works organized by the conductor Alfredo Casella at the Rinnovati theater, one of the oldest in Italy, with members of the press and leading figures in the music world invited with the idea of publicizing its restoration. On this occasion, Pound met Bruno Barilli, the critic and composer, whose work he admired. In *Canto 80* (p.510), he wrote: *"I trust that they have not destroyed the/ old theater/ by restorations, and by late renaissance giribizzi,/ Dove e Barilli?"* Pound had his wish; the theater was subsequently restored without "giribizzi," or unwanted ornamentation; the curved stage was cut back even with the proscenium arch to enlarge space for the orchestra. Olga wrote to Pound at St. Elizabeths: "Barilli turned up after lunch, and I showed him the Cantos & he [was] very pleased to be remembered. He said he had first met you at the Rinnovati, so I showed him how he hooked into that Canto."[32]

Canto 75 is a transcription of the score of the violin part of *La Canzone degli uccelli* (p. 464–5), a choral work by Janequin, arranged for lute in the 16th century by Francesco da Milano and rewritten again for violin (Olga's violin) by Gerhart Munch. The Munch version is reproduced in Olga's hand, signed "Or," and dated September 1933. From an *Il Mare* review, we know that Olga and Munch performed the *Canzone* in concert at Rapallo on November 14, 1933. *Out of Phlegethon* refers to Munch's return to Rapallo on a few days' leave from the "hell" of World War II, when he was called upon to play for the German troops (as mentioned again in *Canto 80: Munch offered Bach to the regiment*[p. 524]).

In *Canto 76*, the poet returns in memory to the stones of Venice, where he wrote *A lume spento,* his first published book: *my window/looked out on the Squiero where Ogni Santi/meets San Trovaso* (p. 476). In another passage, "Unkle George" [Tinkham] "barks" at "the princess" (i.e., Princess Polignac, née Winnaretta Singer). We know that Polignac helped Olga and Pound to secure the Jannequin score mentioned in *Canto 75* because of a December 1933 letter to Olga: "Did Ezra receive Jannequin? That was difficult to find at first."[33] Olga's 1944 diary records: "The Munches arrive the 14th, . . . They and self dine at Palazzo Polignac & play the Chilisotti stuff . . . [Vladimir] Horowitz' remark on hearing M[unch] practice chez moi—*'Ce pianiste joue aussi bien que moi.'* The for Congres Musicale chez P'sse. Present EP, R[ichard] Strauss, Alban Berg, Horowtiz; at P'sse (end of month) to play Lili Boulanger, Bach, . . ."[34]

Olga first went to Venice in the early 1920s to study violin with Bennedetti Marchelli. Pound wrote from Rapallo: "Allright, she GO out and look at Venezia. It will probably improve her playing as much as anything else will. Has she been to S. Giorgio Schiavoni and S. G. dei Graeci, and Sa.M. Miracole? Also *nel* Museo Civico *chi sono qualche cose be'i*; and stick her head back in and out of the window, and NOT fall into the stern chains of the cargo boat just there under the finestra."[35]

In 1928, Olga's American father, J. Edgar Rudge, helped her to buy 252 Calle Querini in Dorsoduro as a real estate investment. From that time, it was her custom to spend later summer and early fall in the "hidden nest" with Pound and their daughter Mary. The house, on a quiet canal near Santa Maria della Salute, had belonged to Gretchen Greene, one-time secretary to Rabindranath Tagore in India. Pound, also a friend of Greene's, knew Tagore during the London years when the Bengali poet's works were being published in English translation with an Introduction by W. B. Yeats (Pound mentions "Rabindranath" in *Canto 77*, p. 488).

Pound's daughter, Mary de Rachewiltz, remembered: "To this house of elegance, tense symbols, charged with learning, wisdom and harmony, I was first brought at the age of four." She remembers "the wall along the stairs leading to the top room was taken up completely by a gray opaque canvas into which I read nothingness, chaos, the universe . . . *Tami's dream,* . . . and on the studio bookcase, *the great Ovid bound in thick wooden boards,* and the *bas-relief of Ixotta* [da Rimini] (*Canto, 76,* p. 476), set in the wall by the desk.[36] The canvas by the Japanese artist, Tami Koume, and the bas-relief were Pound's. He wrote from Rapallo: "She's got the Isotta, which might be put in wall *inside,* but not where the fire wd. smoakk [sic] it."[37]

Also among Mary's childhood memories of the Venice house was the jewel-studded silver bird place on a shelf in Olga's room, a gift from the poet, playwright, and novelist, Gabriele D'Annunzio. D'Annunzio is mentioned twice in this Canto, and again in *Canto 93: there is no doubt that D'Annunzio could move the crowd in a theater* (p. 644). Olga's friendship with the Italian poet dated back to World War I when her younger brother Arthur and D'Annunzio were pilots together: *the holiness of their courage forgotten,* as commemorated by Pound in the Cantos. Arthur was shot down over France and died at 19, but D'Annunzio lived to write a book about his war experiences, and Olga remained his lifelong friend. One of the highlights of her career was a performance at his villa near Verona, the Vittoriale. We know also that Pound had great admiration for the "poet hero"; for example, in *Canto 3,* he refers to "the peacocks in Kore's house," a phrase borrowed from D'Annunzio's Il Notturno.[38]

Pound's relationship with Olga also led to his meeting with Benito Mussolini. Il Duce, himself a violinist of some accomplishment, invited Olga to perform accompanied by Daniele Anfiteatrov at his private residence on the Via Rasella. An article in the Paris edition of the *Herald Tribune* reported: "Mussolini complimented Miss Rudge on her technique and musical feeling, saying that it was rare to find such depth and precision of tone, 'especially in a woman.' He showed his guests the large assortment of violin music on his desk . . . Five violins were on the table in the center of the room, on the best of which the Duce himself plays every evening. After the concert, the Premier offered Miss Rudge a bouquet of magnificent carnations."[39] In spite of Mussolini's heavy features and commanding presence, Olga commented: "he had the manners of an archbishop."

In January 1933, Olga arranged for Pound's audience with Il Duce, who, after reading the *Cantos,* remarked: *ma questo . . . è divertente* (*Canto 41,* p.

202). Mussolini ("the Boss") is also mentioned briefly in *Cantos 74 and 78,* and again in *Canto 87: Why do you want to—perche si vuol mettere—your ideas in order?"/Date '32 (p. 583).* In *Canto 92,* the *"bottai"* who . . . *phoned Torino/ instanter, to dig out Vivaldi* (p. 635) refers to Giuseppi Bottai, Mussolini's Secretary of the Ministry of Corporations, who was called upon to assist Olga and Pound in retrieving the Vivaldi manuscripts from the National Library in Turin. Pound's later involvement with Mussolini's Ministry of Popular Culture (Miniculpop) and the controversial Rome radio broadcasts were to have serious consequences for the poet.

In the last *Cantos,* as in the last years of his life, the poet and the woman who inspired him were drawn ever closer together. *Canto 106* is rich with references to Circe/Olga, harkening back to the beginning of the *Cantos,* with emphasis on Circe's sexuality as a daughter of the Sun: *Circe, Persephone/ so different/ is sea from glen that/ the juniper is her holy bush/ between the two pine trees, not Circe/ but Circe was like that/ coming from the house of smoothe stone* (p. 767). In this *Canto* APHRODITE is linked with EUPLOIA [good voyage], again the wind at the poet's back. In *Canto 114: The kindness, infinite, of her hands . . ./ And that the truth is in kindness* [p. 807] surely referred to Olga, who cared for Pound during his last illnesses. Olga also proofread and prepared for publication the last *Cantos 115–117). Canto 116* refers again to the two places they were happiest together, the island basilica of Torcello near Venice, and the intersection where one could see a cross of blue sky between the buildings in Rapallo: . . . *to affirm the gold thread in the pattern/ (Torcello)* and . . . *al Vicolo d'oro/ Tigullio)* (p. 811).

Beyond civic order: l'AMOR (Canto 94, p. 648) was quoted and under-scored by Olga in her journal, a revealing document that she continued writing into her nineties. Among each day's "noting's down" are significant (to Olga) quotations from the *Cantos* and *Guide to Kulchur* along with hexagrams from the *I Ching.*

Pound mentions the *I Ching* [Book of Changes] in *Canto 53* and again in *Canto 102; 50 more years on the Changes* (p. 743), which is taken from Confucius' saying: "If many years were added to me, I would give fifty to the study of the Book of Changes, and might therefore manage to avoid great mistakes." After Pound joined Olga in 1962, she began throwing the *I Ching* daily for both of them. "These hexagrams have always been made, usually in the morning, first thing after breakfast, . . . commencing with mine, read aloud to Ezra, then his *idem.*"[40]

After Pound's death, Olga continued this practice. On November 14, 1972, she wrote: "She will do it for *Him,* every day as they used to do, hoping he will see & know & influence her throwing for *Him.*" Some of the entries are revealing of both characxters: "EP/ Wei-chi = completion, success; OR/ Chia-Jen = perseverance of the *woman* furthers [OR's emphasis]; EP/ Sun = *the gentle* [OR's emphasis] is able to weigh things, to take spec. circumstances into account; OR/ Ta ch'u = *taming power of the great* [OR's emphasis]." Olga wrote: " 'She' has the feeling that 'He' gets stronger every day." Stronger? His presence nearer? Was Olga receiving a psychic message from her Caro? She faithfully recorded in her journal: "I miss the company of Ezra's silence—am now only happy when alone with thoughts of him . . . [with] love ageless as all eternal things . . . the feeling of 'presence' [is] as intense as at that final hour, the *mutual* awareness which comes and goes, remains . . . as I am writing now (1972)."[41]

In the Addendum for C [100], the poet returns for the last time *dove sta memora,* to Sant' Ambrogio, where the sexton of the old church of San Pantaleo plays Verdi's "La donna e' mobile" [woman is fickle] on the carillon (p. 814). This may have inspird the reflection that, of the many women Pound had known throughout a lifetime, the *exceptional* woman was Olga Rudge, who never wavered in caring for him. In a letter to Mary from St. Elizabeths in 1945, the poet wrote: "Dearest child: Tell your mother I bless the day I first saw her, & thank her for all the happiness she has brought me—a gleam of hope now the sun is reborn" (referring to the birth of his first grandchild). In a postscript he added: "First, one must go the road to hell & to the bower of Circe's daughter" (*Canto 47*)."[42]

NOTES

NOTE: Page numbers of passages quoted in the text are from *The Cantos of Ezra Pound* (New York, New Directions, 1989 ed.) All quotations from the Rudge/Pound Correspondence are located in chronological order in Olga Rudge Papers (Series I: Correspondence), Beinecke Rare Book & Manuscript Library, Yale Collection of American Literature.

1. OR to Caresse Crosby (Sept. 7, 1965). Special Collections, Morris Library, Southern Illinois University at Carbondale.

2. EP to OR (Oct. 2, 1925).

3. EP to OR (Jan 23, 1930).

4. "Through Alien Eyes," *NA* (Feb. 6, 1913).

5. OR to EP (Oct. 10, 1961).

6. OR to Peter Dale Scott, Berkeley, CA (Oct. 12, 1985).

7. *NA* (Nov. 25, 1920).

8. George Antheil, *Bad Boy of Music* (London, Hurst & Blackett, 1947), p.99.

9. *PM* (London, Peter Oliver, 1962), p. 39.

10. *See* Translation & Postscript of Remy de Gourmont, *The Natural Philosophy of Love* (New York, Boni & Liveright, 1922), cited by E. Fuller Torrey, *The Roots of Treason* (New York, McGraw-Hill, 1984).

11. OR Papers (Series III; Notebooks), Beinecke.

12. *Odyssey*, X, 221–23.

13. "Poets in Paradise," *The Listener* (Jan. 5, 1956), quoted by Michael Reck, *Ezra Pound* (New York, McGraw-Hill, 1984), p. 145.

14. *See* Bowen, *Drawn from Life* (New York, Virago, 1984), p. 145.

15. OR Papers (Series III: Notebooks), Beinecke.

16. Ibid.

17. Letters of EP, ed. D.D. Paige, No. 348, in Ezra Pound Collection, Beinecke.

18. OR Papers (Series III: Notebooks), Beinecke.

19. Mary de Rachewiltz, *Discretions* (New York, Atlantic/Little Brown, 1971), p. 117.

20. OR Papers (Series III: Notebooks), Beinecke.

21. M.de Rachewiltz, *Discretions*, p. 258.

22. Ibid., p. 190.

23. OR Papers (Series III: Letterbook, 1945), Beinecke.

24. EP to OR (June 20, 1948).

25. OR to EP (Sept. 4, 1948).

26. *Guide to Kulchur* (London, Faber & Faber, 1938), p.9.

27. OR to EP (Feb. 14, 1948).

28. Chigi to OR (Jan.9, 1943), Accademia Musicale Chigiana Archives.

29. OR to EP (July 30, 1937).

30. M.de Rachewiltz, *Discretions*, pp. 132–33.

31. OR to EP (Feb. 27, 1937).

32. OR to EP (Sept. 19, 1948).

33. Polignac to OR, OR Papers (Series II: General Correspondence)

34. OR Papers (Series III: Notebooks), Beinecke.

35. EP to OR (Oct. 22, 1924).

36. M. de Rachewiltz, *Discretions,* p. 22.

37. EP to OR (Sept. 12, 1928).

38. Pound reviewed *Il Notturno* in *The Dial* (Oct. 1922).

39. *Herald Tribune*, Paris ed. (Feb. 25,. 1927).

40. OR Papers (Series III: I Ching Notebooks, 1966–1986).

41. Ibid.

42. EP to M. de R., OR Papers (Series II: General Correspondence).

3

MASSIMO PESARESI

Ezra Pound, a Poet from Hellas:
the Dionysian Persona

The Hellenic legacy is primarily the legacy of myth. Like history, myth is rewritten by each generation, accordding to its needs, beliefs, and aesthetic sensibility. In our time, this recreation of ancient mythology has often focused on one god: Dionysus. An eccentric figure in the Greek pantheon, Dionysus was believed to be a foreign deity, coming to Hellas from afar (Thrace, Asia Minor, or India—there is even a clay tablet found in the palace of Nestor on which the name of the god appears in the genitive form as Di-wo-nu-so-jo). Nietzsche's interpretation of Greek tragedy and the related polarity of the Apollonian and the Dionysian still shapes our view of Hellas.[1] In Germany, however, Dionysus had already been a key figure in poetic and philosophical speculation. Hölderlin, in particular, had developed a myth in which the wine-god is a symbol of the redeeming powers of man, often embodied by the act of poetry: Dionysus is a savior, on a par with Heracles and Christ, and belongs to the world of demigods, a step or two below the Olympian majesty of Apollo or "Vater Aether."

An ideal kinship between Dionysus and Christ was already foreshadowed in classical antiquity, and during the Middle Ages the topos of *Christus patients,* or The Passion of Christ, was often compared with the "passion" of Dionysus; the two figures were eventually paired by German Baroque authors (such as, for instance, Hugo Grotius, who dwells on the theme of "Christus und Dionysos als Leidende"[2], or Martin Opitz' translation of Danielis Heinsius' hymns to Christ and Bacchus)[3]. In our century, Dionysus, though disregarded by Sigmund Freud (who as the mythographer of psychoanalysis made extensive use of Greek myth), nevertheless became the object of extensive scholarly studies.[4] Less fortunate among poets, the Greek god was overshadowed sometimes (for example, in Rilke's *Sonnets to Orpheus*) by his Thracian follower, Orpheus.

But Pound, a champion of the permanence of the pagan spirit amidst the barbarism of *usura,* often converses with Dionysus in the *Cantos*, and so makes him into his own persona, as hero and martyr. Inheriting the syncretism of late antiquity, Pound equated Dionysus with mythical figures such as Iacchus, Bacchus, and Zagreus, who eventually became merged with the wine-god, and Pound tended to use these names interchangeably.

In *Canto 2,* Pound condensed the narrative (based on the Homeric hymn and on Ovid's *Metamorphoses*) of Dionysus' first frightening epiphany aboard a slave ship, where he converted the ship into a vineyard, and the epithet of "Lyaceus" is attached to him. There is a famous vase painting by Exekias of this Dionysian episode on a cup from Vulci, which is now in Munich. *Lyaios* or *Lysaios,* namely "the one who delivers from suffering", is an attribute that emphasizes the soteriological aspect of the god, a Christian interpretation of Dionysus which the German philosopher Friedrich Schelling used as early as 1804.[5]

Another Dionysian name is Iacchus, which appears twice (in Greek script, once in the nominative, once in the vocative) in *Canto 79,* in the context of vegetation rituals, marked with the almost obsessive refrain of the invocation to the lynx: "Lynx, my love, my lovely lynx." *Iakchos* was originally the hymn sung by the devotees at Eleusis, as is mentioned by Herodotus in his history, and by Aristophanes in one of his comedies, and the word derives from *iakhe,* "noise": the Iakchos was later personified by Strabo as "Archegetes", the god, or hero, that leads the cortege. The similarity of the terms Iakchos and Bakchos (which designated the participant in the orgiastic rituals) contributed to the identification of Iacchus and Dionysus by Sophocles in his *Antigone,* a specifically Athenian identification. Such an identification is also connected with the presence of Dionysus in the Eleusinian mysteries, for which a passage from Pindar's VII Isthmian Ode provides the earliest testimony. He praises "The long-haired Dionysus, who sits next to Demeter of the bronze cymbals" (ll. 4–5). Against the skepticism of many scholars, P. Foucart[6] has convincingly documented the presence of Dionysus at Eleusis, and put forth the interesting hypothesis that the god presided over the highest contemplative moment of the mysteries, the *epopteia,* while Demeter was prominent in the preceding phase of the ritual. This chthonic aspect of the god (venerated as the son of Persephone) is echoed, in the Poundian passage, by the references to Kore (the "maiden" par excellence, an autonomastic designation of Demeter's daughter), Demeter herself ("Keep from Demeter's furrow"), and Pomona, the pomegranate ("Melagrana or the Pomegranate field"), an unmistakable attribute of Persephone.[7] In this Dionysian context the Christian invocation of mercy appears: "*eleeson* Kyrie eleison / each under his fig tree / or with the smell of fig leaves burning," as Pound writes in *Canto 79,* acknowledging that the fig tree is sacred to Dionysus. It may be interesting to note—although the coincidence can hardly derive from such a reference—that in the Second Council of Constantinople, in 691, it was ordered that the wine-treaders should cry "kyrie eleison" whenever a load of grapes was brought in, instead of their traditional invocation "Dionysos."

Connected with Iacchus is the name Bacchus, at least in Pound's view. The link is provided by the passage in Alexander Del Mar's *History of Monetary Systems* (quoted in the *Companion to the Cantos of Ezra Pound*) which was the source of the phrase "a golden Bacchus on your abacus" (97:685): "besants are [. . . .] called Iaku of gold [. . .] *iaku* being the Hebrew form of the Greek

Iacchus and Roman Bacchus."[8] A pre-Hellenic word, Bakchos is probably related to Lydian *baki* "child" (an element that stresses the image of Dionysus as Urkind or Divine Child.) Used as an epithet of the god as participant in the rite, it became a name of his; in Euripides' fragment 477, we read the invocation : "O lord Bacchus, lover of the laurel tree, O Paean Apollo, skilled in lyre playing".[9] Originally, *Bakchos* probably referred to the twigs, or branches carried by the initiated.[10]

Zagreus seems to be the most privileged Dionysian name in the *Cantos*. In one of the latest fragments (*Notes for CXVII* et seq.), Pound mentions "an altar to Zagreus / Son of Semele." The same phrase ("over an altar to Zagreus") occurs in *Canto 105* with reference to the king of the Franks, Pepin (751–768), who was crowned over an altar to Zagreus at the church of St. Denis in Paris, as Pound notes in *Canto 95*: "(vine-leaf? San Denys/(spelled Dionisio)/Dionisio et Eleutherio." The name, framed by the two replicas of the Chinese ideogram *ch'eng* (explained as "perfect or foetus" in the list appended to the canto) closes *Canto 77,* and as an invocation ("Zagreus, Io Zagreus") resounds in the opening of *Canto 17,* the celebration of Dionysus' abundant fertility, framed by the enigmatic setting of Venice, Greece, and Provence.

A powerful chthonic god of Cretan origin, connected with lordship over wild beasts, Zagreus is invoked, together with the Earth goddess in the lost epic poem *Alcmaeonis*; he is son of Hades according to a fragmentary play by Aeschylus, and of Persephone, according to Callimachus. The god was later identified with Dionysus, probably following Orphic influence. When this identification took place is still a controversial issue.[11] It is clearly attested for the first time in the 3rd century B. C. in a Callimachus fragment (43.117), quoted in the *Etymologicum Magnum*: "Zagreus is Dionysus among poets: it seems, in fact, that Zeus mated with Persephone, by whom the chthonic Dionysus was born. Callimachus says: . . . the daughter that gave birth to Dionysus Zagreus,"[12] but it may go as far back as the 5th century B.C., on the basis of a passage from Euripides' lost tragedy *Cretan Men*: "I became an initiate of Zeus Idaeus, and experiencing the ways of the night-wandering Zagreus, and the banquets of raw flesh, and lifting the torches of the Mountain Mother, among the Kouretes, once purified I received the name of Bacchus."[13] Although some scholars (Nilsson, among others) are inclined to refute such an early identification, Giorgio Colli, on the authority of Guthrie, provides some stringent arguments on the Dionysian character of a few elements in Euripides' quoted fragment (such as, for instance, the passing reference to *omophagia*). The name Zagreus has no certain etymology but seems to be related to the sphere of hunting: in Greek, a hunter who catches living animals is called Zagreus. Later scholars interpret the name as "great hunter" by analogy with *zatheos* "thoroughly divine" [. . .] But the Ionian word *zagre*, [. . .] signifying "pit for the capture of live animals,' proves that the name contains within it the root of *zoe* and of *zoon*, "life" and "living thing." An exact translation of "Zagreus" would be "catcher of game."[14] Although it is not clear why Pound preferred this Dionysian name over the other ones, he was perhaps aware of the original meaning of Zagreus as "catcher of live animals," as it appears from the context in which the word first occurs in the *Cantos*: "chirr—chirr—chir-rikk—a purring sound, / And the birds sleepily in the branches, / ZAGREUS, IO ZAGREUS!" (*Canto* 17) Less ambiguous, however, is the fact that Zagreus became a mythical persona of the poet: an identification possibly favored by the belief that Dionysus' birthday coincided with the poet's own birthday.[15]

The most powerful Dionysian figure in the *Cantos*, however, is *Digonos*. The term, which refers to the double birth of the god, was probably familiar to Pound from an anonymous epigram in the *Greek Anthology*, containing the epithets of Dionysus in alphabetical order.[16] However, Pound knew that in the Orphic Hymns, Dionysus was referred to as "Trigonos," or "thrice born," and also as "Dimator" or "the one with two mothers," and it was his own deliberate choice to identify him as "twice born."

The passage in *Canto 48*, inserted in a section dealing with the involvement of the Jews in World War I, is rather obscure: "Digonos / DIGONOS; lost in the forest; but are then known as leopards / after three years in the forest; they are known as 'twice-born.' " It has been noted by his daughter Mary[17] that Frobenius suggested to Pound a relationship between the myth of Dionysus and African rituals of rebirth, and the source of the term *Digonos* may well be Frobenius' *African Genesis*.[18] The connection of panther and leopard with the Dionysian sphere is clear and well documented in classical texts, as we know from the leopard skin worn by Dionysus in Euripides' tragedy of the *Bacchae*. Furthermore, a significant connection of the panther with rebirth can be found in *Canto 72*, one of the Italian Cantos:

> Così puoi rinascere, così diventare pantera,
> Così puoi conoscere la bi-nascita, e morir una seconda volta.

> (Thus to be born again, thus to become panther,
> Thus to know rebirth, and to die a second time.)

In the above passage of *Canto 48*, however, a reference can be seen to cult societies of wild hunters, who on certain occasions identified themselves with beasts of prey. An interesting page in Jane Ellen Harrison's *Prolegomena to the Study of Greek Religion* (Cambridge, 1903, pp. 484 ff.) may have given Pound such a suggestion. Commenting on Firmicus Maternus' description of a Cretan sacrifice, the British scholar emphasizes the connection between that remnant of Dionysian *omophagia* and the ritual killing and dismemberment of a camel among Sinaitic Arabs in the fourth century of the Common Era. Her account of the sacrifice relies on a passage in Nilus Ancyranus' *Narratio*, already referred to by William Robertson Smith, who, in his *Lectures on the Religion of the Semites*, summarizes the Greek text with the following words:

> [. . .] the camel chosen as the victim is bound upon a rude altar of stones piled together, and when the leader of the band has thrice led the worshippers round the altar in a solemn procession accompanied with chants, he inflicts the first wound, while the last words of the hymn are still upon the lips of the congregation, and in all haste drinks of the blood that gushes forth. Forthwith the whole company fall on the victim with their swords, hacking off pieces of the quivering flesh and devouring them raw with such wild haste, that in the short interval between the rise of the day star which marked the hour for the service to begin, and the disappearance of its rays before the rising sun, the entire camel, body and bones, skin, blood and entrails, is wholly devoured.[19]

Regardless of the different angles from which Nilus' account was viewed, it may be worth remarking the rather uncanny fate that the story had over the centuries. Uncanny it seems, in fact, that the horrified report of pagan customs provided by a pious hermit at the close of antiquity impressed the mind of a Scottish Catholic scholar (whose orthodoxy had already been questioned in heresy trials) and, through the latter's words, stirred the imagination of an agnostic Jew, intent on laying the foundations of a secular genesis.[20]

The fire in which the *Pisan Cantos* were molded transfigured the erudite quotation into a majestic and tragic symbol: "DIGONOS, but the twice crucified / where in history will you find it?" (*Canto* 74: 439). The historical reference is to the gruesome epilogue of Fascism: Benito Mussolini and his lover, Claretta Petacci, murdered and hung by the feet from a scaffold in Piazzale Loreto, at Milan, on April 27, 1945. More complex is the genealogy of Pound's myth. The analogy of Dionysus and Christ goes back to the historical and religious roots of Western civilization, and as some mythologists have noted, both the founding of Christianity and what can be subsumed under the comprehensive term "Dionysian religion" emerged from a common background: the Mediterranean wine-culture. One need only think of the many metaphors that Jesus Christ took from the life of the vine-growers, just as the Hebrew prophets had done before him: "I am the vine and the branches," etc.

In modern European literature, the Nietzschean association of Dionysus and Christ is ambiguous and emblematic. At the end of Nietzsche's *Ecce Homo*, the phrase "Dionysos *gegen* den Gekreuzigten" ("Dionysus *against* the Crucifixion") appears, while the last notes which Nietzsche sent to Cosima-Ariadne are signed "Dionysos, der Gekreuzigte" (i.e., "Dionysus, the Crucified"). The opposition or the identification of Dionysus and Christ are sealed with a sign of martyrdom: unlike the triumphant brotherhood intimated by Hölderlin, the Nietzschean pair is marked by a penitential aura, characteristic of the Christian spirit so violently abhorred, at times, by the philosopher.

In view of this opposition, it seems strange that an author blessed with a pagan soul, as Ezra Pound certainly was, would have contaminated his own glorious persona, Dionysus, with the image of the cross. It should not be forgotten, however, that Dionysus was, at least in the Orphic tradition, a god that dies: as a child, he was torn to pieces by the Titans. This was the *sparagmos* or dismemberment, an integral part of the Dionysian ritual: in their frenzy, the Maenads used to tear apart live animals, and in some cases even humans (like Pentheus). The Dionysian ritual of dismemberment and eating of raw flesh (*omophagia*) is commemorated in Euripides' *Bacchae*, and there are many references elsewhere, among Classical authors such as Plutarch, to the murderous, destructive (and self-destructive) nature of man. The symbolism of sacrificial killing reveals a dark side of Greek myth, which emerges from the feral character of *homo necans*. When these seeds of guilt, present in the Hellenic soil, came in contact with Judaic severity and sternness, some ghastly fruits ripened: the life-negating forces of Christian mortification. Apart from such historical and social developments, the sinister and barbarous elements of the Hellenic imagination, so uncannily remote from the touch of tenderness, can still coalesce into grim shapes in a poet's mind. It is not surprising, then, that even Ezra Pound, the chanter of the Eleusinian splendor, in the direst storm of his life, should have resorted to such appalling symbols of human (and divine) suffering as Dionysus offered him to represent an overwhelming historical and personal tragedy.

NOTES

1. Although anticipated by Friedrich Creuzer, *Symbolik und Mythologie der alten Völker, besonders der Griechen* (4 vols. 2nd Ed. Leipzig-Darmstadt, 1819–1821. III: 164–168), the opposition of the two gods became paradigmatic in Nietzsche's philosophy for the first time.

2. Cf. Lothar Kempter, *Hölderlin und die Mythologie.* (Wege zur Dichtung, 6. Nendeln/Liechtenstein, 1971), p. 149.

3. Opitz' "Lobgesang Bacchi" und "Lobgesang Christi" can be found in *Gesammelte Werke* (Ed. George Schulz-Behrend, Vol. 2, Stuttgart, 1978) pp. 11–44. Novalis also used such telling phrases as "Xstliche Dithyramben und Lieder" and "die Xstliche Semele" (with reference to Mary) in his *Schriften,* (Ed. Paul Kluckhohn and Richard Samuel, Stuttgart, 1965, Vol. III: 591, Nr. 239).

4. See, for instance, Walter Friedrich Otto, *Dionysos: Mythos and Kultus,* (Frankfurt, 1933), Henri Jeanmarie, *Dionysos: Histoire du culte de Bacchus* (Paris: Payot, 1951), Martin Persson Nilsson, *The Dionysiac Mysteries of the Hellenistic and Roman Age* (Lund, 1957), and Karl Kerényi, *Dionysos, Urbild des unzerstörbaren Lebens* (München—Wien, 1976).

5. Cf. *Werke* (Ed. Manfred Schröter. 7 vols. München, 1927–1959) I/6, 66, 67 ff.

6. *Les Mystères d'Eleusis.* Paris, 1914.

7. For the connection of Dionysus with pomegranate, see Clemens Alexandrinus: *"ek tôn toû Dionusou aimatos stagonôn beblastêkenai nomizousi tas roias"* ("they believe that pomegranates were formed from the blood drops of Dionysus"} (*Protreptikon* II, 19).

8. Alexander Del Mar, *History of Monetary Systems* (Chicago, 1896) pp. 212–213.

9. Cf. A. Nauck *Tragicorum Graecorum Fragmenta: Supplementum adiecit B. Snell,* Hildesheim, 1964.

10. Cf. Xenophanes, fr. 17, (H. Diels and W. Kranz, *Die Fragmente der Vorsokratiker,* I-III, Berlin, 1951–52).

11. See M. P. Nilsson, *The Minoan-Mycenaean Religion and its Survival in Greek Religion* (2nd Ed. Lund, 1968 (1950)) pp. 578–581; and W. K. C. Guthrie, *Orpheus and Greek Religion* (2nd Ed. London, 1952).

12. *Etymologicum Magnum* (Ed. T. Gaisdorf. Oxford, 1848) p. 406, 46.

13. The passage is quoted in Porphyry's *De abstinentia*, 4, 19.

14. "Karl Kerényi, *Dionysos: Archetypal Image of Indestructible Life.* (Trans. Ralph Manheim. Princeton: Princeton U P, 1976) p. 82.

15. Cf. *The Little Review* 8.2 (Spring 1922) p. 40.

16. *The Greek Anthology.* (Trans. W. R. Paton. The Loeb Classical Library. Cambridge, Mass.: Harvard U P—London: Heinemann, 1958) III: 289–290.

17. "Fu Frobenius a indicare a P. le corrispondenze fra i riti dionisiaci e certe credenze africane legate alla rinascita." (Ezra Pound. *I Cantos*. Ed. by Mary de Rachewiltz. Mondadori: Milano, 1985: p. 1536).

18. For instance, in *A Companion to the Cantos of Ezra Pound* (Vol. 2: 301), we find among the sources of Canto 74 (in which the word Digonos appears again) *African Genesis* (1937), by Leo Frobenius and Douglas Fox (reissued by Benjamin Blom. New York, 1966).

19. *Lectures on the Religion of the Semites. The Fundamental Institutions.* With an Introduction and Additional Notes by Stanley A. Cook, and a Prolegomenon by James Muilenberg (Ktav Publishing House: 1969) p. 338.

20. Robertson Smith's passage is quoted in Freud's *Totem and Taboo* (*The Standard Edition of the Complete Psychological Works of Sigmund Freud.* Trans. by James Strachey. Hogarth: London, 1958. Vol. 13: 138).

4

ALAN PEACOCK
Pound, Catullus and Imagism

Peter Whigham has noted how "it is well known that round about 1914–16 Pound, Hulme, Ford and others were of the opinion that English verse was in need of certain qualities, such as hardness, clarity and directness, which are usually associated with epigrammatic technique."[1] He observes how Pound turned to Catullus for this quality, rather than to the Greek tradition, because he was not "Swinburnian," in Pound's term. Whigham concurs in this distinction: "it is true that the actual verbal structure of Greek does tend towards the allusive. The acme of finality is to be found in Roman rather than Greek epigram. There you have hardness and weight together."[2] The Latin scholar Kenneth Quinn, looking at things from a classicist standpoint, has similarly observed how Pound, in some poems in *Personae*, strikes a recognizably Catullan note.[3] Catullus of course appears regularly in Pound's prose writings as an exemplar of certain kinds of excellence. The fact of the Catullan influence, then, is plain; and in what follows I wish to look at specific instances of it in action in Pound's work in the early Imagist and pre-Imagist period, and then make some observations on the gains thereby, both in terms of Pound's own output and of the early development of Imagism.

One thing which has to be noted at the outset is the limited direct creative pay-off for Pound in terms of specific poems which may be termed successfully Catullan in tone or style. For in spite of the constant enthusiasm that Pound shows for Catullus in his prose writings, where the key words are always along the lines of his "cleanness," "directness," and "hardness," the actual influence on Pound's own poetry is often oblique and sometimes oddly desultory. There is in fact only a limited engagement with Catullus in terms of translation, and in his imitative activity Pound does not notably reproduce the strengths of Catullus (as he views them in the prose criticism). A good example of this rather tangential approach is "Blandula, Tenulla, Vagula." Pound's poem takes up and develops certain promptings from Catullus 31 in a very surprising and idiosyncratic way.

Catullus' poem is written in affectionate celebration of his longed-for Sirmio (modern Sirmione on Lake Garda, the location of his villa) as he greets it like a special friend (or, perhaps, retainer) after time spent on duties abroad:

> . . . quam te libenter quamque laetus inviso,

49

> vix mi ipse credens Thyniam atque Bithynos
> liquisse campos et videre te in tuto.
> o quid solutis est beatius curis,
> cum mens onus reponit, ac peregrino
> labore fessi venimus larem ad nostrum
> desideratoque acquiescimus lecto?
> hoc est, quod unumst pro laboribus tantis.
> salve, o venusta Sirmio atque ero gaude
> gaudente; vosque, o Lydiae lacus undae,
> ridete quicquid est domi cachinnorum.

(" . . . with what joy I revisit you, scarcely trusting myself that I have left Thynia and the Bithynian plains, and that I see you in safety. Ah, what is more blessed than to put cares away, when the mind lays by its burden, and tired with labour of far travel we have come to our own home and rest on the couch we longed for? This it is which alone is worth all these toils. Welcome, lovely Sirmio, and rejoice in your master's joy, and you, ye waters of the Lydian lake, laugh out aloud all the laughter you have in your home.")[4]

Compare Pound:

> What hast thou, O my soul, with paradise?
> Will we not rather, when our freedom's won
> Get us to some clear place wherein the sun
> Lets drift in on us through the olive leaves
> A liquid glory? If at Sirmio,
> My soul, I meet thee, when this life's outrun,
> Will we not find some headland consecrated
> By aery apostles of terrene delight,
> Will not our cult be founded on the waves,
> Clear sapphire, cobalt, cyanine,
> On triune azures, the impalpable
> Mirrors unstill of the eternal change?[5]

Clearly a sea-change has occurred, in terms which are signalled by the title of Pound's poem which is an adaptation of the emperor Hadrian's poetic address to his own soul ("Animula vagula blandula..":[6] "O little soul, fleeting and lovely"). Catullus' personal poem of topographical association has taken on metaphysical dimensions. The journey evoked in Catullus' poem, back from his duties in Bithynia, becomes life's journey; and Sirmio (in Catullus simply the loved location of his villa) is now envisaged as the ideal spiritual locale where the soul may finally find peace. A strong parallelism is maintained by Pound. There is the same sense of well-deserved rest (''when our freedom's won'') as in Catullus' poem and a similar stress on the welcoming topography of Sirmio and the waves of Lake Garda. But the Catullan material, so warmly affectionate and anthropomorphic in its celebration of Sirmio (''salve'' is a human greeting), suffers a profound revision when filtered through the supervening metaphysical sentiments.

The fact is that in ''Blandula, Tenulla, Vagula'' Pound makes his approach to Catullus not as a translator or imitator but by wide-ranging literary and topographical association. Hardy had visited Sirmione and produced appropriate Catullan reflections in ''Catullus: XXXI. (After passing Sirmione, April 1887),'' and so had Tennyson.[7] As Hugh Kenner and Donald Davie have indicated,[8] Garda and Sirmio are to be regarded as ''sacred places'' for Pound, and it is for this reason presumably that they can provide a fulcrum for metaphysical reverie in the adaptation of Catullus' poem. Certainly the area has an imaginative hold on Pound: Garda (Benacus in the Latin) is featured in ''The Flame'' (''Sapphire Benacus, in thy mists and thee / Nature herself's turned metaphysical . . . ''); and later, in ''The Study in Aesthetics,'' Sirmione figures in a passing Catullan reference.[9]

Drastically reworked topographical reference (rather than stylistic emulation) is again the connective element in another notably divergent Catullan adaptation. In ''Phasellus Ille'' in *Ripostes* Pound offers a literary squib based on Catullus 4, where the Latin poet evokes, via a dedicatory tribute to his pinnace (the *phasellus* of Pound's title), the sights seen in his journeying back from his Bithynian sojourn to Lake Garda. Pound's opening picks up the first two lines of Catullus' elaborately evocative lyric:

> This *papier-mache*, which you see, my friends,
> Saith 'twas the worthiest of editors.
> Its mind was made up in 'the seventies',
> Nor hath it ever since changed that concoction.[10]

This determinedly travesties Catullus' poem:

> Phaselus ille quem videtis, hospites,
> ait fuisse navium celerrimus,
> neque ullius natantis impetum trabis
> nequisse praeter ire, sive palmulis

opus foret volare sive linteo.

("The pinnace you see, my friends, says that she was once the fleetest of ships, and that there was never any timber afloat whose speed she was not able to pass, whether she would fly with oar-blades or with canvas.")[11]

The Catullan basis of Pound's satirical squib is clear—as is also the notable divergence from the invoked precedent. In the course of his poem Pound does preserve a sense of the Catullan original behind it by, for instance, the reference to the "horrid threats of Bernard Shaw" (cf. "horridamque Thraciam / Propontida": " ... the wild Thracian Propontis"); by "Twould not move it one jot from left to right" (cf. "laeva sive dextera / vocaret aura": "whether the breeze from left or right invited"); and by the mention of the Cyclades which figure largely in Catullus' poem. But the contact is one-dimensional: the reader may enjoy an amusing sense of recognition in Pound's satirical juxtaposition of ancient and modern and the disparity of content and sentiment between the poems; but little more than that. The question therefore arises as to how we are to take Pound's classicising here. Intimate familiarity with Catullus is evident, but why is Catullus' complex and artful poem so desultorily invoked?

Of course, it may be said, that is precisely the point: Catullus' highly suggestive, linguistically complex and formally structured (it is in the form of a grave-epigram) poem becomes, appropriately for Pound's satiric target, a lacklustre, truncated put-down—a kind of epigrammatic equivalent to the deliberate bathos of the mock-heroic. Hence too, Pound's archaizing ("saith 'twas") might be seen as a consciously banal equivalent for certain mannered stylistic effects in Catullus: "Saith 'twas ... " in fact corresponds to the (rare in Latin) Greek "nominative and infinitive" construction of "ait fuisse navium celerrimus" in Catullus. Witness too in Catullus the "Ennian" compound epithet in *buxifer* and the exotic place-names and lively word-play as where the Dioscuri, Castor and Pollux, are apostrophized as "gemmelle Castor et gemmelle Castoris" ("twin Castor and Castor's twin'). His poem is laden with touches of this kind of delicate, learned playfulness; and Pound, as was said, may be writing his poem as a managed exercise in comprehensive disparity.

The probable and straightforward answer is, though, that Pound is not so much taking close cognizance in this way of the Latin and its linguistic exoticisms as haphazardly pastiching phrases from a familiar poem which simply surface in the memory. The poem, it is suggested, is the same sort of exercise and shows a similar order of aesthetic achievement as the Yeatsian pastiche, "The Lake Isle," in *Lustra*:

O God, O Venus, O Mercury, patron of thieves,
Give me in due time, I beseech you, a little tobacco-shop,
With the little bright boxes
       piled up neatly upon the shelves . . . [12]

And so on. Details such as "And the whores dropping in for a word or two in passing" indicate clearly the parodic intentions of Pound's urban re-run of Yeats's familiar sentiments. The minimal contact with Yeats is sufficient for the poem's limited strategy. "Phasellus Ille," with its more extensive run of verbal correspondences might seem to hesitate between this sort of effect and that of a more elaborately worked spoof. I would suggest, though, that the way in, which the Catullan material surfaces in "Phasellus Ille" in an insistent, but aesthetically limited, way is a good illustration of the distinction to be made between evidence of familiarity with and respect for Catullus in Pound on the one hand and direct profit in terms of creative imitation on the other. The latter is extremely variable and, as was said, at times desultory.

With *Lustra*, for instance, we are immediately pointed in the direction of Catullus, as the interrogative first line of Catullus' first, dedicatory poem—

Cui dono lepidum novum libellum . . . ?
(To whom am I to present my pretty new book?)

is changed into a relative clause for Pound's

Vail de Lencour

Cui dono lepidum novum libellum[13]

and we find a direct engagement with a Catullan poem in "To Formianus' Young Lady Friend," subtitled "after Valerius Catullus":

All Hail! young lady with a nose
       by no means too small,
With a foot unbeautiful
       and with eyes that are not black,
With fingers that are not long, and with a mouth undry,
And with a tongue by no means too elegant,
You are the friend of Formianus, the vendor of cosmetics,
And they call you beautiful in the province,
And you are even compared to Lesbia.
O most unfortunate age![14]

This close version of Catullus 43 avoids archaism (seen in other epigrams in the volume) and is reminiscent of the effort to make the Classics unfussily and unpedantically available in translation in the *Egoist* project of 1915. Coming, as it does, close after "Papyrus," it certainly underlines Pound's tendency in this period towards a type of epigram which subsumes both Greek and Roman sources. If we look around however for further examples of special indebtedness to Catullus in particular, the gleanings are thin. "The Study in Aesthetics" is, for Whigham, "singularly reminiscent of No. 42 of the *Carmina*, while the two poems I should choose to place beside Nos. 38 and 46 . . . are 'The Garret' . . . and 'The Gypsy':

> That was the top of the walk, when he said:
> "Have you seen any others, any of our lot,
> "With apes or bears?"
>   —A brown upstanding fellow
> Not like the half-castes,
>   up on the wet road near Clermont.
> The wind came, and the rain,
> And mist clotted about the trees in the valley,
> And I'd the long ways behind me,
>   gray Arles and Beaucaire,
> And he said, "Have you seen any of our lot?"
> I'd seen a lot of his lot . . .
>   ever since Rhodez,
> Coming down from the fair
>   of St. John,
> With caravans, but never an ape or a bear.

Both the Latin and the English achieve that curious blend of the direct and the allusive which it seems to me are among Catullus' and Pound's more distinctive attributes."[15]

  Whatever the truth of the general impression recorded by Whigham here, there is little in his cited comparisons which can be pinpointed to illustrate a clear indebtedness to Catullus specifically. Both "The Gypsy" and Catullus 46 are about journeying (46 anticipates his departure home from Bithynia and the sights to be seen en route), and "The Study in Aesthetics" does, as was noted above, mention Catullus and Sirmione; but, amidst the generalized Greco-Roman debt of the run of Pound's epigrammatic poems of this period, it is difficult to isolate any striking Catullan indebtedness. Catullus is one of a number of Latin poets to whom reference is made.

  "Prayer for his Lady's Life" is a well-known version of Propertius,[16] and Tibullus, Propertius' fellow love elegist, receives an allusion to his most famous line in "Impressions of Francois-Marie Arouet (de Voltaire)":

And Tibullus could say of his death, in his Latin:
"Delia, I would look on you, dying."[17]

This picks up Tibullus, 1,1:

> te spectem, suprema mihi cum venerit hora;
> te teneam moriens deficiente manu.

> (May I look on thee when my last hour comes; may I
> clutch thee, as I die, with failing grasp.)[18]

More obliquely in the same poem, the section "To Madame Lullin," in which
the line just quoted appears, may owe something to Tibullus' "nos, Delia, amoris
/ exemplum cana simus uterque coma." ("but let us twain still be pattern lovers
when our hair is white") at the end of I,6:[19]

> You'll wonder that an old man of eighty
> Can go on writing you verses . . .
> Grass showing under the snow,
> Birds singing in the late year!

> And Tibullus could say of his death, in his Latin:
> 'Delia, I would look on you, dying.'

> And Delia herself fading out,
> Forgetting even her own beauty.

Similarly, Horace's famous *Odes* III, 30 provides the title of "Dum Capitolium
Scandet" and the germ of its sentiment—just as it does the title "Monumentum
Aere, etc." in *Poems from Blast*.[20] In neither of these cases is there any significant
development of the Horatian connection; and generally in Pound's dealings with
the Roman poets during these years the impression is of constant nodding in the
direction of the more familiar figures of classical Roman poetry, with an emphasis on their more familiar poems. In all this, the Catullanizing does not stand
out as a particular area of especially fruitful indebtedness.

This of course bears out what Pound has to say in *ABC of Reading* about
Catullus' intractability for the translator: "I personally have been reduced to
setting them [Villon and Catullus] to music as I cannot translate them."[21] I refer
again therefore to the distinction which must be made between Catullus as a
direct imitative model, and as an exemplar of style. For it is in this latter connection that Pound keeps harking back to him in his criticism. Catullus, whatever
the difficulty about translating him, is constantly in Pound's mind during the

years in which *Personae*, *Ripostes* and *Lustra* were produced. These were of course the same years in which Pound was effecting his Imagist revolution. Moreover, there is a remarkable coincidence between Catullus' distinctive qualities (as Pound sees them: see above) and the stylistic desiderata articulated while Imagism was being concocted and then promulgated. It is this correlation which is explored in what follows.

******

In F.S. Flint's famous account of "Imagisme" in *Poetry* (1913),[22] the "Imagistes" are initially described in negative and rather conservative terms: they "admitted that they were contemporaries of the Post-Impressionists and the Futurists; but they had nothing in common with these schools. They had not published a manifesto. They were not a revolutionary school . . . ''; and amidst all this rather vague information as to what they (whoever "they" are) are not about (surely an ironic, bantering vagueness?) we are given the certainly less than revolutionary information that "their only endeavour was to write in accordance with the best tradition, as they found it in the best writers of all time—in Sappho, Catullus, Villon." The classical emphasis is striking—as is the fact that the exemplars offered by the anonymous "Imagiste" from whom Flint affects to glean his information happen so exactly to correspond with Pound's favorite trio. We are given of course the Imagists' famous "few rules, drawn up for their own satisfaction only":

> 1. Direct treatment of the 'thing,' whether subjective or objective.
> 2. To use absolutely no word that did not contribute to the presentation.
> 3. As regarding rhythm: to compose in sequence of the musical phrase, not in sequence of a metronome.

Now, directness, terseness, expressive rhythm and metre—all these are what many would see as Catullan and, more generally perhaps, "classical." There is added of course the mysterious " 'Doctrine of the Image', which they had not committed to writing; they said that it did not concern the public, and would provoke useless discussion." While holding back on these *arcana* (the only ones, it may be observed, which might justify their title!) the "Imagistes" would instruct poetasters by the following stunts:

> 1. They showed him his own thought already splendidly expressed in some classic (and the school musters altogether a most formidable erudition).

2. They re-wrote his verses before his eyes, using about ten words to his fifty.

What more mainstream neoclassical pitch is conceivable?

Two years before, in 1911, T.E. Hulme had looked forward to "a period of dry hard classical verse"[23] (23) as a corrective to sentimentality. Pound's use of Greco-Roman models during the Imagist period and in particular his admiration for Catullus as an exemplar of hardness, clarity, and directness in poetry is an integral aspect of a more diffused current of opinion and aspiration. In his 1915 article, "The History of Imagism," Flint traces the provenance of the school back to 1909 when he and T.E. Hulme, after the latter's split with the Poets' Club of 1908, initiated the proto-Imagist gatherings, joined by Pound in 1909. He records, significantly, that "Ezra Pound used to boast in those days that he was *Nil praeter "Villon" et doctus cantare Catullum . . .*"[24] Flint seems to take this slogan, together with Pound's fascination with troubadour poetry, as evidence of a rather backward-looking, traditionalist theoretical position on Pound's part at this point: "He could not be made to believe that there was any French poetry after Ronsard. He was very full of his *troubadours*; but I do not remember that he did more than attempt to illustrate (or refute) our theories occasionally with their example." In fact, though, in styling himself as "schooled to sing nothing beyond Villon and Catullus," Pound is picking up Horace's gibe against poets of his day in Augustan Rome whom he sees as "nil praeter Calvum et doctus cantare Catullum."[25] In context, the adjectival phrase relates specifically to "simius iste": "that ape, schooled to sing nothing beyond Calvus and Catullus." Horace is targeting his contemporaries who follow the so-called New Poets (*poetae novi*) of the previous generation at Rome, of whom Catullus is the representative. In reversing Horace's gibe, then, and applying it in *positive* terms to himself, Pound is, as Flint sees, invoking the classical past—but specifically revolutionary and, as we might say, "modernist" elements of that past. (There is a further piquancy in the fact that the "ape" whose place Pound willingly takes in the revised quotation may well be none other than Propertius!) At any rate, Catullus' importance for Pound during this period is emphasized. He is an authoritative exemplar of certain "classical" qualities which go towards defining stylistic and theoretical priorities which flow into the tenets of Imagism as originally formulated.

The theoretical, almost talismanic importance of Catullus to Pound should be understood in these terms. And his appreciation of the Latin poet is only sharpened by practical attempts, as we have seen, to import some of Catullus' qualities into his own writing. In this latter connection, though, it has to be freely conceded that the process is very much a hit-and-miss affair. Pound is often ordinary in an area of literature where Catullus excelled:

This thing, that hath a code and not a core,

> Hath set acquaintance where might be affections,
> And nothing now
> > Disturbeth his reflections.

> > > ("An Object")[26]

And one can set the stubborn archaising tendency of this against the attempt to achieve impact by over-directness in *Poems from Blast*:

> . . . Here is the taste of my boot
> Caress it,
> > lick off the blacking.

> > > ("Salutation the Third")[27]

> . . . And it is doubtful if even your manure will be rich
> > enough
> To keep grass
> Over your grave.
> > > ("Monumentum aere, etc.")[28] (28)

In such cases, Pound demonstrates problems with idiom and a heavy-handedness which leave it clear that Catullus, for all Pound's admiration of him, could never be his literary *alter ego* as Horace was to Ben Jonson or Propertius proved for Pound. His importance, over an extended period, is as a touchstone of style and excellence rather than as a direct model.

****

Beyond this, I hope that it is becoming apparent that the early theory and practice of Imagism are inextricably bound up with an important pre-First World War strain of neo-classicism. A sense of tradition and an impulse towards reform and renewal are, at least within the coterie orchestrated by Pound, held in exemplary balance. It is notable, for instance, how many classical translations are included in the Imagist output. The idea of the Classics as a testing-ground for the avant-garde, the practical interaction in these terms of traditionalism and innovation, is clearly of great importance for the later achievement of high modernism; and it is this symptomatic and corrective aspect of Imagism that I wish to emphasize.

What I want to stress is that the desiderata for the release of the potency of the "Image" are synonymous with the delivery of English poetic style and diction from a verbose and inert late-Romantic, late-Victorian legacy. Moreover, as I have tried to suggest, the early dynamics of this process reside not so much in the development of an essentialist concept of the image as in a neo-classical clearing away of dead wood. The emphasis is formal rather than metaphysical. The Image, that is to say, had to be released in formal terms before it could be aggrandized by accentuation or pursued as a projective, dynamic credo.

Pound's 1914 essay on Vorticism in the *Fortnightly Review*, of course, provides this new emphasis, quoting from Flint's 1913 formulations, but now insisting that the image "is a radiant node or cluster; it is what I can, and must perforce, call a VORTEX . . . "[29] This whirls us immediately beyond the neoclassical contexts which I have been elaborating. The redefinition of the image as "a radiant node or cluster . . . through which and into which, ideas are constantly rushing . . . " helps to elucidate the previous 1913 formulation of "A few don'ts," where "An image is that which presents an intellectual and emotional complex in an instant of time" and how Pound could shift immediately into the asseveration that "the presentation of such a 'complex' " can give "that sense of sudden liberation; that sense of freedom from time limits and space limits: that sense of sudden growth, which we experience in the presence of the greatest works of art."[30] Within the essentially neoclassical disciplines of the earliest phase of Imagism (as adumbrated in the Flint/Pound article), these momentous ideas remain relatively undeveloped. In the "Vorticism" article however they are richly and discursively contextualized within Pound's more insistent concern with the status of the image and, by extension, the work of art. The pivot here of course is away from neoclassical stylistics and towards post-Romantic theory and, as I said, my focus is essentially on the former.

In fact, Pound himself does not trade in these particular distinctions in this matter. When he wishes, for instance, to cite an example of an extended Imagist poem, he notes that "Dante's *Paradiso* is the most wonderful *image*."[31] It is a literary-historical outlook that allows Pound to pursue his consistent conviction that literature is a continuum—that innovation may to an extent be a matter of rediscovery. Certainly, Pound's attitude to, and use of, Catullus exemplifies how innovatory or reforming movements in literary style and practice may also be, in many ways, acts of reclamation. Committed as Pound was, and in terms critically formulated as early as *The Spirit of Romance* (1910), to the idea of tradition where "all ages are contemporaneous" and where an ideal literary scholarship "will weigh Theocritus and Yeats with one balance,"[32] he assimilates the example of Catullus in terms of contemporary relevance. The "masterwork" never becomes out of date in this sense. Past lessons may need to be relearned, and corrective exemplars endure in what T.S. Eliot terms an "ideal order."[33] The literary products of the present must be read and evaluated simultaneously with the legacy of previous tradition. As Pound puts it in "Vorticism," "We do not desire to evade comparison with the past. We prefer that the comparison be made by some intelligent person whose idea of 'the tradition' is not limited by the conventional taste of four or five centuries and one continent.''[34] With this in mind, then, I would like to take up Pound's archetypal imagist poem, "In a Station of the Metro"—

> The apparition of these faces in the crowd;
> Petals on a wet, black bough.[35]—

and look at two other floral images to illustrate both the process of "release" that I have been stressing, and the kind of self-sufficient, creative dynamism that the image can provide. At the same time a further reconciliation between ancient and modern may be suggested in this latter respect.

F.S. Flint's own work, as it appears for instance in the July 1909 issue of *The English Review*,[36] notably utilizes archaising vocabulary in the production of its rapt, unworldly, mystical tone:

> Say, were it not more meet
> To sandal you with poppies for shoon,
> And of the sacred moon
> A ghostly wafer eat?
>
> Think! how ardent and discreet
> Would your bearing be,
> Your bosom burning white in monstrancy,
> And wise your feet.
>   ("A Poet Advises His Lady")

The last line, a collector's item in bathos, shows the dangers of this style. The Yeatsian "He Likens Her to a Rose-Tree, Himself to the Wind" however is more successful:

> Our feet are treading on earth's parapet
> Over the heavens; among the stars we slept.
>
> The night is all before us, far and fair,
> And the four winds play in our ruffled hair.
>
> Along the black bare branch sleeps almond-bloom,
> Silvery in the slow silver of the moon.
>
> You are mysterious, and you speak no word;
> And who you may be I have never heard . . . [37]

Within the rapt, stellar incantation is the image of the almond blossom on the "black bare branch," allowed to stand juxtapositionally with its referent, the "you" of the poem. The effect is comparable with Pound's "Petals on a wet, black bough" in "In a Station of the Metro'—if we except, of course, the anthropomorphism in "sleeps" and the Yeatsian repetition in "silvery" and "silver." Not that one should necessarily wish them away: they are appropriate to the conception of the poem. My point is simply the embedding of the image amongst other things. The rise of imagism is in essence a matter of revised priorities. The essentials were always there, waiting to be released again. Pound's famous use of the scissors to produce "In a Station of the Metro" merely dramatizes this fact graphically.

Let us however give the last word, or the last image, to Catullus. In Poem 11, addressing his acquaintances Furius and Aurelius on the subject of Lesbia's unfaithfulness in the most trenchant terms (which illustrate everything I was saying earlier about his command of conversational inflexion and idiom), he finally characterizes the nature of his sense of injustice:

> cum suis vivat valeatque moechis,
> quos simul complexa tenet trecentos,
> nullum amans vere, sed identidem omnium
>   ilia rumpens.
>
> nec meum respectet, ut ante, amorem,
> qui illius culpa cecidit velut prati
> ultimi flos, praeter eunte postquam
>   tactus aratrost.

("Bid her live and be happy with her paramours, three hundred of whom she holds at once in her embrace, not loving one of them really, but again and again draining the strength of all. And let her not look to find my love, as before; my love, which by her fault has dropped, like a flower on the meadow's edge, when it has been touched by the plough passing by.")[38]

In order to gloss such an effect, we need to proceed beyond the Imagist desiderata recorded by Flint in 1913 to the heuristic dynamism and self-sufficiency with which Pound credits the image from his 1914 Vorticist perspective:

> All poetic language is the language of exploration. Since the beginning of bad writing, writers have used images as ornaments. The point of Imagisme is that it does not use images

as ornaments. The image is itself the speech. The image is the
word beyond formulated language.[39]

The essential consideration is not the formal relationship between image and
referent, but the complex new thing which comes into existence in a passage
such as that quoted.

Within the simultaneous order of past and present masterworks and past
and present thinking about them, not only can the past illumine the present, but
also vice-versa; and it is in the kind of language which Pound employs in his
developed concept of the image that we begin to find a vocabulary to do justice
to Catullus' use of the image: "The image is not an idea. It is a radiant node or
cluster; it is what I can, and must perforce, call a VORTEX, from which, and
through which, and into which, ideas are constantly rushing." Catullus' image
is a formal simile, but just as surely as Pound's image in "In a Station of the
Metro," it breaks down any simplistic interpretation of the image in terms of
ornament and mere analogy.

Such observations, of course, take us beyond the question of the Catullan
(and by extension Classical) influence on Pound's style and theory in the early
Imagist (or pre-Vorticist) period. This was the focus of the present article. It is
valuable however to note how Pound's developing thinking on the image expands
to a point where it is serviceable for such far-ranging comparisons. This however
is possible only after the essential, corrective ground-clearing exercise within
the, in many ways, neoclassical phase of Imagism which the present article has
sought to elucidate.

NOTES

1. Peter Whigham, 'Ezra Pound and Catullus' in *Ezra Pound: Perspectives*, ed. Noel Stock (Chicago, Henry Regnery, 1965), p.64.

2. Ibid., p.65.

3. Cf. Kenneth Quinn, *Catullus: An Interpretation* (London: Batsford, 1972), p.25. He notes epigrammatic poems in *Personae* which are a 'conscious pastiche' of Catullan poems and which 'depend on our recognition that this *is* pastiche.'

4. *Catullus, Tibullus, Pervigilium Veneris*, trans. F.W. Cornish, J.P. Postgate and J.W. Mackail, 2nd edn., revised G.P. Goold, Loeb Classical Library (Cambridge Mass., Harvard University Press, 1988), pp. 36–7. Hereafter referred to as "Goold."

5. *Personae: Collected Shorter Poems of Ezra Pound* (London, Faber and Faber, 1952), p.53.

6. *Scriptores Historiae Augustae*, Vol. I, trans D. Magie, Loeb Classical Library (Cambridge, Mass., Harvard University Press, 1921), p.78.

7. Cf. *Collected Poems of Thomas Hardy*, 4th edn. (London, MacMillan, 1930), p.166; "Frater Ave atque Vale," *The Poems of Tennyson*, ed. Christopher Ricks (London, Longmans, 1969), p. 1284.

8. Hugh Kenner, *The Pound Era* (London, Faber and Faber, 1972), p. 322; Donald Davie, *Pound* (London, Fontana, 1975), p.30.

9. *Personae*, pp. 64 and 105.

10. Ibid., p. 75.

11. Goold, pp. 4–7.

12. *Personae*, p. 128.

13. Ibid., p. 90.

14. Ibid., p. 123.

15. Whigham, pp. 73–74.

16. *Personae*, p. 32: cf. Propertius II, 28, 47–56.

17. *Personae*, p. 178.

18. Goold, pp. 196–97.

19. Ibid. pp. 228–29.

20. *Personae*, pp. 105 and 158.

21. Ezra Pound, *ABC of Reading* (London, Faber and Faber, 1951), pp. 104–05.

22. F.S. Flint, 'Imagisme', *Poetry*, Vol. I (1913), excerpted by J.P. Sullivan, *Penguin Critical Anthologies: Pound* (Harmondsworth, Penguin Books, 1970), pp. 40–41.

23. Quoted by Peter Brooker, *A Student's Guide to the Selected Poems of Ezra Pound* (London, Faber and Faber, 1979), p. 61.

24. F.S. Flint, 'The History of Imagism', *The Egoist*, Vol II, No. 5, May 1st, 1915, p. 71.

25. Horace, *Satires* I, 10, 18–19: *The Satires of Horace*, ed. A. Palmer (London, MacMillan, 1883), p. 49.

26. *Personae*, p. 76.

27. Ibid., p. 158.

28. Ibid.

29. Sullivan, p. 57.

30. Ibid., pp. 41–42.

31. Ibid. p. 31.

32. Ezra Pound, *The Spirit of Romance* (London, Peter Owen, revised edn. 1970), p. 8.

33. T.S. Eliot, 'Tradition and the Individual Talent' in *The Sacred Wood: Essays on Poetry and Criticism*, University Paperbacks edn. (London, Methuen, 1960), p. 50.

34. Sullivan, p. 55.

35. *Personae*, p. 119.

36. 'A Poet Advises his Lady', from 'The Net of the Stars' by F.S. Flint, *The English Review*, Vol. II, No. 8, July 1909, pp. 638–42. See p. 638.

37. Ibid., p. 640.

28. Goold, pp. 16–17.

39. Sullivan, p. 53.

5

PHILIP GROVER
Ezra Pound, Eleanor d'Aquitaine and Her Troubadours

The mortuary statue of Eleanor is quite remarkable. I know no other medieval statue like it. She is there at Fontevraud with her husband, Henry II, and her son, Richard I, the Lion-Hearted. Their statues are those of kings, with their scepters and their crowns. They are interchangeable. There are slight variations in the drapery, in the position of the hands, the inclination of the heads on the cushions, but the faces are indistinguishable. They are the stock in trade for the faces of kings—or at least what the sculptors at Fontevraud had in their stock for the Plantagenets. But Eleanor is different, and not just because she is a woman. She carries no royal insignia except a crown, but above all she is given a personal attribute of immense significance: she is reading a book. Yes, her eyes are closed, but then this is a mortuary statue. There are other statues of men holding books, but never *reading* them. And these men are prophets or evangelists and the book quite obviously is the Bible: the Bible is as important as, or more important than, the person holding the book. And it is a traditional, stereotypical symbol. But not the book that Eleanor is reading: it is by no means obvious what the book is. What is important is that she is defined as a woman who reads: this is the attribute which the sculptor wishes to perpetuate, by which he wanted posterity to remember Eleanor. This is a woman for whom literature is one of the central activities of her life, for whom books and reading are the primary attributes by which she is to be understood. No other queen of England or France is ever understood or depicted in these terms.

What book is she reading? Pious, *bien-pensant* French Catholic historians have lately argued that it is a religious work, a book of piety. Well, perhaps. Eleanor did retire to Fontevraud which was a monastery, but retiring to a monastery, particularly if you were rich and powerful, did not carry with it the necessity of great religious fervor. And certainly the writers whom she encouraged or whom she gathered around her in her lifetime were not religious writers but poets, troubadours, or the first "novelists" like Chrétien de Troyes. She is also the dedicatee of Wace's *Brut*—the French translation of Geoffrey of Monmouth's legendary history of British kings—as well as Benoit de Sainte-Maure's *Roman de Troie*. In her meet the two contending languages of North and South France: *langue d'oc* and *langue d'oil*—and three cultures. Since she is buried in a monastery, those who wish may see her act as one of piety, while those who reflect on her highly secular life and recall her importance as a patron and

subject of erotic poetry are free to interpret the book in a different way: quite
appropriately, the sculptor has made his symbol ambivalent and ambiguous.

As far as Ezra Pound is concerned, Eleanor first appears in *Canto VI*, a
Canto framed by a reference at the beginning to Odysseus and at the end by
one to Theseus. But the Canto itself is one that treats principally with the
troubadour tradition, starting with the first troubadour, Guillaume d'Aquitaine
(Seventh of Poitiers, Ninth of Aquitaine), Eleanor's grandfather, and including
references to Eleanor's two husbands, Louis VII of France and Henry II of
England, her escape from numerous suitors after her divorce from Louis and
before her marriage to Henry, her reputed (but fictitious) escapade with Saladin
and her too close relationship—again reputed—with her uncle in Acre, which
is supposed to have prompted the celebrated sestina by Arnaut Daniel—the first
ever—with its play on *oncle, ongla*. And there is a long section—long by
Pound's Canto standards—about Eleanor and Bernart de Ventadorn, with an
imaginary conversation between the two partly based on lines from Bernart's
cansos.

La Vida de Bernart says that after he was expelled from Ventadorn
because the *vescoms*, Ebles III, had perceived that he and the viscountess were
lovers:

> 'El . . . s'anet en Normandia, a la duchessa q'era adonc domna
> dels Normans, et era joves e gaia e de gran valor e de prez e
> de gran poder, et endendia mout en honor et en prez. Et ella
> lo receub con gran plaiser e con grant honor e fo mout alegra
> e la soa venguda e fetz lo seignor e maistre de tota la soa cort.
> Et enaissi con el s'enamoret ede la moillier de so seignor,
> enaissi s'enamoret de la duchessa, et ella de lui. Lonc temps
> ac gran joia d'ella e gran benanansa, entro qu'ella tolc lo rei
> Enric d'Angleterra per marit e qe lan mena outra lo brac del
> mar d'Angleterra, si q'el no la vi mai, ni so mesatge. Don el,
> puois, de duol e de tristessa qe ac de lei, si se fetz monges en
> l'abaia de Dalon, et aqui persevera tro a la fin.

> ["He went to Normandy, and the duchess was there the lady
> of the Normans and was young and gay and of great worth
> and distinction and great power and she was well versed in
> matters of honour and merit. And she received him with great
> pleasure and great honour and was very delighted with his
> arrival and made him the lord and master of all her court. And
> as he had fallen in love with the wife of his lord so he fell in
> love with the duchess, and she with him. For a long time he
> had great joy and happiness with her till she took the King of

England for husband and he led her across the arm of the sea
to England so that he saw her not again nor her messenger.
Therefore he subsequently, from the suffering and sadness he
had from her, became a monk at the Abbey of Dalon and there
he remained to the end.''']

Eleanor's place in the literary life of her time has been well treated by
Rita Lejeune and it is not my purpose to repeat her work. Besides being the
granddaughter of the first troubadour, Guillaume IX of Aquitaine, she was the
patron of many poets and even the subject of a song in the *Carmina Burana*—in
German. Besides Bernart de Ventadorn and Bertran de Born who were closely
connected with either her court or the courts of her sons, let me mention briefly
that in addition to the two *planhs* for the Young English King written by Bertran
de Born, only one of which seems to have interested Pound, another troubadour,
Cercamon, wrote a *planh* on the death of her father Guillaume X—which death
precipitated her marriage to Louis VII at the age of fifteen (or perhaps seven-
teen)—and another, Gaucelm Faidit, wrote a *planh* on the death of her favorite
son, Richard. This poem is said by his modern editor to be his most famous
work. Such was the cultural milieu of this remarkable woman.

Pound often uses the *vidas* and *razos* of the troubadours quite uncritically.
For example, the famous Maeuz (or Maheut or Maent) of Montignac ''n'a jamais
existé, de meme que son prétendu mari, Talairan, frère du comte de Périgord''
[''never existed any more than her pretended husband, Talairan, brother of the
Count of Périgord''].[1] It is not even modern erudition which has undermined
this lovely legend; it was already undermined in Pound's time. And the most
recent editor of Bertran de Born, Gérard Gourian, in his massive critical edition
in two volumes adds that:

> Depuis que Stronski a démontré que l'ignorance de l'auteur
> des razos était si totale, en ce qui concerne du moins les amours
> de Bertran, qu'il était allé jusqu'à inventer de toutes pi le
> personnage de Maheut de Montignac, il faut bien renoncer à
> croire à son superbe roman qui lui permettait de lier entre elles
> des huit poésies amoureuses de Bertran de Born.[2]

> [''Since Stronski has demonstrated that the ignorance of the
> author of the razos was so total, at least as far as the loves of
> Bertran are concerned, that he even went as far as to invent
> totally the personage of Maheut de Montignac, we must give
> up believing in his superb novel which allowed him to link
> together the eight love poems of Bertran de Born.'']

But if this is the case, what happens to our understanding of Part I of "Near Périgord"? For at the start of Part II, Pound writes "End fact. Try fiction." We have already been deep in fiction, beginning with Maent. Of course, Bertran did write the poems alluded to, but he never mentions Maent in his poems: this is a name supplied by the razos.[3]

The *vidas* and *razos* are full of facts which are nothing but fictions: surely we do not accept that all we have to do is to read a poem or novel and deduce the lives of the authors from them. But that is often the level of historical or literary criticism in these *vidas*. It is now generally accepted—and accepted in Pound's day, too—that about the only reliable things in the *vidas* and *razos* were the names, places of origin, and social conditions of the poets, and not even always these, as shown in the case of Cercamon, for example, whose name is deduced from the supposed fact that he travelled much in the world: Cercamon. Pound is often quite dismissive of historical objections, as if he did not want his favorite beliefs and stories questioned. Of course, one can go on using fictions as fictions, knowing they are such, even when their historical truth is denied, but it would appear that Pound did not want to accept the fictionality of what was presented to him as history. When he and Dorothy visited Hautefort and Montignac in August, 1919, Dorothy sent a postcard of the castle of Hautefort to her mother from Montignac, on the back of which she wrote: "This is where Bertran de Born's 'Maent' lived. Last night we slept close to where Henry II's men probably camped, besieging B. de Born." So Pound either knew that Maent was a total fiction and ignored it to the point of forgetting to mention the fact to his wife, or he ignored the evidence that already challenged the *vidas*. In any case, it illustrates something important, to me at least, about the way Pound operates in the *Cantos*. Pound declared that an epic is a poem containing history: no, for Pound it is a poem with *stories* in it: history, or legend, or myth, or other fictions. Once in the poem, the distinction between history and story, truth and fiction is lost. Such practice is all right, as long as you do not pretend you are presenting history with the aim of correcting it, or using it to instruct the reader in true government.

Similar amalgamations between history and legend, or refusals to make distinctions, happen with Pound's treatment of Eleanor.

> As she rode out to the palm-grove
> Her scarf in Saladin's cimier
>
> (*Canto VI*)

is pure fiction. And what is striking about this fiction for Pound is that the source(s) are ecclesiastical, and from those who have a vested interest in blackening Eleanor's reputation. When he came to Malatesta and similar libels on his good name, whose sources are again ecclesiastical, Pound is ready to defend Sigismondo and set the record straight. Two observations: Eleanor is a woman, and she is not therefore such an important hero in his panoply; in fact, are any women the sources of more than erotic importance to Pound? Eleanor *could* have been: he however amalgamates her into the eternal Helen figure, and her historical importance and her immense personal political activity are lost sight of. And because her importance is erotic and as an exemplar of the Provencal love tradition, it does not matter that she has been libelled as having affairs with her uncle and a young Arab boy not yet sexually mature: her free loving is what is to be celebrated even if it never existed. Eleanor indeed is viewed quite differently by the poets and the writers of the *vidas* and *razos*—who sometimes were poets or jongleurs themselves, as in the case of Uc St. Circ—and the chroniclers who were almost always clerics. For the poets and jongleurs she was "joves e gaia e de gran valor e de prez e de gran poder, et endia mout en honor et en prez." And she was a great and important patron of poets, one of the greatest of her time, if not indeed the greatest.

    Canto VI continues the themes found in the previous troubadour Canto, *Canto IV*. The central theme is erotic love as celebrated and practiced by the troubadours. Guillaume of Poitiers is recognized as the originator of the troubadour tradition, as the "finder' of the mode and the inventor of "fin amour," the concept of "courtly love" as practiced by the troubadours, although a distinction is often made between the "fin amour" of the troubadours and "courtly love." Thus in *Canto VIII*:

> And Poictiers, you know, Guillaume Poictiers,
>   had brought the song up out of Spain
> with the singers and viels

Canto VIII, p. 32

This being the case, that is, that Guillaume is the first of the troubadours and the first to introduce a whole new repertory of themes and poetic forms, indeed the founder of the modern European secular love lyric, it is quite surprising, to say the least, to notice the lines by him which Pound quotes:

> 'Tant las fotei com auzirets
> Cen e quatre vingt et veit vetz . . . '

> ["So many times I fucked them as you shall hear:
> one hundred and eighty-eight times!"]

This is hardly the language of "fin amour," and the stanza continues with:

> Q'a pauc no'i rompei mos coretz
> E mos arnes'

["That I nearly broke my straps and my harness"]

Obviously this image has to be understood metaphorically. This poem does not form part of Guillaume's courtly love poetry: it belongs to an entirely different genre: it is a "gab," a boastful tall-story, and fiercely anti-clerical as well as scurrilous and bawdy. The language even has embarrassed French critics: Jeanroy in his 1913 edition (which presumably Pound knew) refused to translate this stanza. And more recently René Labande[4] states that even in Latin such things are unrepeatable! Why does Pound include these in many ways unrepresentative lines; unrepresentative at least of the new mode of Western secular love poetry that is the troubadour tradition of which Guillaume is the undisputed originator? One clue may be in the next line of the Canto which celebrates fecundity:

> The stone is alive in my hand, the crops
> will be thick in my death year.

Another reason may be that Pound wants us to realize the full range of sexual sentiments, the noble and the gross, the refined and the bawdy. After all, these are possible in the same mind: we have the superb example of Shakespeare. Perhaps for Pound part of what Provence celebrates is this intense love of life which excludes nothing in its joy, its jouissance. For Provence certainly for Pound was a complete civilization.

The phrase "domna jauzionda" is both a frequent one in Provencal poetry and one to be found in Bernart de Ventadorn's poem beginning "Tant ai mo cor ple de joya" which is thought by more than one critic to be addressed to or at least to refer to Eleanor.[5] For instance, Carroll Terrell[6] sees the poem as addressed to Eleanor on her return to Poitiers after her divorce from Louis, but the lines

> Mo cor ai pres d'amor
> que l'esperitz li cor,
> mas lo cors es sai, alhor,
> lonh de leis, en Fransa.

hardly square with that interpretation, since the poet laments that he is here in France while his lady is elsewhere. His heart and spirit are there, but his body is elsewhere, far from her, in France. So in the next stanza he wishes to be a swallow so that in the depth of night he might fly to her and enter her "repaire," her retreat. It is in this stanza that he calls her "domna jauzionda"—a line full of assonance and internal rhyme so that the phrase is emphasized as no other in the whole stanza: "Bona domna jauzionda" and "jauzionda" itself rhyme with three other central words: "ironda," "prionda," and "fonda": the desire to be with her in the depth of night expresses a love so great that unless it is requited his body will "fonda": melt, dissolve, be destroyed.

> Ai Deus! car no sui ironda,
>   que voles per l'aire
> e vengues de noih prionda,
>   lai dins so repaire?
> Bona domna jauzionda,
>   mor se l'vostr' amaire!
> Paor ai que'l cors me fonda,
>   s'aissi'm dura gaire.
>   Domna, per vostr'amor
>   jonh las mas et ador!
> Gens cors ab frescha color,
>   gran mal me faitz traire!

["Ah God! why am I not a swallow which flies through the air and comes in the profound night there within her repair? Good joyful lady, your lover is dying! I fear me that my body will melt away if this goes on any longer. Lady, for your love I join my hands and adore. Gracious person of fresh hues (colors) you cause me great suffering!]

But was even this canso written about or to Eleanor? It is highly doubtful, but by the use Pound made of it in *Canto VI* it would appear that he thought it did.

A certain number of Bernart's songs were composed in England at the court of Eleanor and Henry II, and he was in England at Henry's court because he had been at Eleanor's court in Poitiers and Normandy before. Henry himself would not have taken him on his own. As Appel remarked long ago, Provencal poetry did not find a durable shelter at the court of Henry II. Bernart is the only troubadour of whom we know with certainty that he spent some time in England.[7] Some songs such as "lancan vei per mei la landa" (Appel, no. 26; Lazar, no. 29) make a direct reference to his stay in England, while the song "Pel doutz chan que'l rossinhol fai" (Appel, no. 33; Lazar, no. 10) is dedicated to, or at least addressed to, Eleanor, "la reina dels Normans":

Lancan vei per mei landa

> Faihz es lo vers tot a randa,
> si que motz no'l deschapadolha
> outra la terra normanda,
> part la fera mar prionda . . .
>
> Si'l reis engles e'l ducs Normans
> o vol, eu la veirai abans
> que l'iverns nos sobreprenda.
>
> Pel rei sui engles e normans
> e si no fos Mos Azimans
> restera tro part calenda.

> ["The verse is made all of a piece, so that not
> a word is out of place, beyond the Norman land,
> on the other side of the deep savage sea . . . If
> the English king and the Norman duke wish it, I
> shall see her before winter overtakes us. By
> the king am I English and Norman, and if it were
> not for my Magnet I would stay here until after
> Christmas."]

It has been suggested that the poem beginning "Chantars no pot gaire valer" may also have been written for or to Eleanor. Even if this poem has no direct connection with Eleanor, it has an importance in the development of the Provençal conception of love. Thus stanza V of "Chantars no pot gaire valer" reads:

> En agradar et en voler
> es l'amors de dos fis amans.
> Nula res no i pot pro tener,
> Si'lh voluntatz no es egaus.
> E cel es be fols naturaus
> que do so que vol, la repren
> e'lh lauza so que no'lh es gen.

> ["In reciprocal pleasure and desire is the love of two
> noble lovers. It profits not lest their wills are the
> same. And he is a born fool who reprehends love for
> that which it seeks and praises it for what is not
> appropriate to it." Free translation: Lazar thinks
> "la" refers to the "domna."]

Pound's version reads:

> 'Tis not a game that plays at mates and mating,
> Provence knew;
> 'Tis not a game of barter, lands and houses,
> Provence knew.
> We who are wise beyond your dream of wisdom,
> Drink our immortal moments; we 'pass through.'
> We have gone forth beyond your bonds and borders,
> Provence knew . . .

Another troubadour even more closely linked with the Plantagenets and Eleanor's children is Bertran de Born; but then his domain lay within the duchy of Aquitaine and he was their liege. Gerard Gourian, in his magisterial edition of de Born, states that in February, 1173, Henry II brought Richard, Coeur de Lion, Geoffrey, Duke of Brittany, King Alfonso of Spain, and Count Raimond of Toulouse all together at Limoges. It was the last time that Eleanor and Henry held court together. For the occasion, Bertran wrote a *canso* directed at Geoffrey of Brittany, "Rassa, tant creis e mont'e poia." (No. 1, pp. 11–35) "Rassa" means "conspiracy" and the *raso* tells us that this was the nickname that Bertran and Geoffrey directed at each other. The *raso* for the *canso* states that Geoffrey, Richard Coeur de Lion, as well as King Alfonso of Aragon and Count Raimond of Toulouse all presented themselves as suitors to Bertran de Born's lady, Maheut de Montignac! And Bertran wrote this *sirventes* to warn them off and convince them that she had granted all her favors to him. Gourian takes the piece as court entertainment; after all, Geoffrey is only just fourteen. But that is just the age when one begins to become sexually active, as the current jargon has it. And there is nothing puritanical or hypocritical about the recognition of sexuality in the secular poetry of the troubadours, though it may have been the case with the Church. Indeed, this is just one aspect of the ongoing struggles for dominance between the poets and the clerics.

Bertran and his *planh* for the young English king both have an important place in Pound's work. "Si tuit le dolh elh planh elh marrimen" is one of Pound's recurrent leitmotivs, a cultural touchstone, a luminous moment, a vortex of thought and emotion. Pound uses it as a phrase to evoke all the emotions and circumstances of the original poem and one which can be used in analogous circumstances to draw comparisons and enhance the meaning of the moment. (What happens to lyric poetry when Pound quotes it in a narrative context? What is the relation between quotation and other poetry, or between quotations? How does the meaning of the original change within the new context?) Hence at the end of *Canto LXXX* we hear again the voice of Bertran de Born, but now invested with Pound's lament and sadness and pain, for it comes at the end of a long Canto which recounts the loss and death of his friends and the life and values which Pound has cherished. Bertran speaks for Pound and Pound takes on Bertran's voice and lament for his own, thus fusing the two losses, the two "complaints," in the medieval sense. And because Bertran lamented the loss of a Plantagenet Pound plays on that—"for the leopards and broom plants"—turning it into a dirge for the death of England, an England that was feudal, royal, aristocratic, and full of blood, the leopards and the broom plants being a metonymy for the whole line of English kings at least to William and Mary:

> Tudor indeed is gone and every rose,
> Blood-red, blanch-white that in the sunset glows
> Cries: "Blood, Blood, Blood!" against the gothic stone
> Of England, as the Howard or Boleyn knows.
> ....
> and God knows what else is left of our London
> my London, your London.

What was the lament of a twelfth-century poet for the death of a young future Plantagenet king becomes also the lament of a twentieth-century poet for the loss of a world he has known, and in part at least imagined, and for the loss of particular friends. The Provençal words have become a universal talisman, a transhistorical summation of a universal sentiment which can be recreated in new circumstances, and by being restated, the present becomes imbued with an historical weight and meaning it would otherwise lack, and the past becomes revitalized by expressing the present. This happens again at the beginning of *Canto LXXXIV*:

> 8th October:
> Si tuit li dolh elh plor
> Angold Τεθνηκε
> tuit lo pro, tuit lo bes
>
> Angold Τεθνηκε

There is however the interesting addition in that "tuit lo pro, tuit lo bes" do not occur in either of the laments for Young Henry: these would seem to be Pound's additions in the spirit of the elegies and now specifically applied to Angold. But since these eulogies are expressed in Provençal, they implicitly, by the context, invoke the praise of Bertran for Young Henry and raise Angold to the status of a medieval knight, if not even to the equal of a future king! Pound's aristocracy is very Jeffersonian: an aristocracy of worth.

There are a number of *sirventes* directly related to de Born's struggles with Richard, particularly over the control of Hautefort, for in his struggles with his brother Constantin, Richard supported the latter. Therefore, not surprisingly, the *sirventes* "Corz e gestas e joi d'amor" is addressed to the Young King for aid against Richard. (No. 15, pp. 271–93) The *sirventes* "Un sirventes que motz no-ill faill" also deals with the struggles between de Born and Richard. Here he tells us that:

> Tot lo sen ai dinz lo seraill,
> Si tot m'an donat gran treball
> Entre N'Azemar e-N Richart (lines 9–11)

["I've all my wits about me, even though between them Lord Richard and Lord Aimar have given me a lot of trouble."]

And a little later he depicts his struggles and all the evils his enemies inflict upon him:

> Tot jorn contendi e-m baraill
> M'escrime e-m defen e-m tartaill
> E-m fon om ma tera e la m'art
> E-m fa de mos arbres issart
>   E mescla-l gran en la pailla,
> E non ai ardit ni coart
>   Enemic qu'er no m'assailla. (lines 22–28)

["All day long I struggle and fight/Wield my sword and defend myself and lay about me/And they ruin and burn my land/And lay waste my woods/And mix the straw with the grain/And I have no enemy however brave or cowardly that does not attack me."]

Pound was familiar with this *sirventes*, for it supplies the epigraph to "Near Perigord": "A Peiragours, pres del muraill." (l. 43) Another *canso*, "Be-m platz lo gais temps de pascor"—which from this opening line might well sing of love, and indeed it does, but not the love for a woman but instead Bertran's love of war—contains another phrase often repeated by Pound: "E (y) cavals armatz." This catch-phrase then switches us into the whole military-aristocratic ethos so fiercely defended and celebrated by Bertran, for example in the stanza:

> Qui que fassa de bos issartz,
> Eu me sui totz temps mes en grans

Cum puosca aver cairels e dartz,
Elms et aubercs, cavals e brans
C'ab aisso-m conort
E-m teing a deport
Assaut e tornei
Donar e dompnei

["Let he who wishes clear away his trees; I have always made
an effort so that I could have bolts and arrows, heaumes and
hauberts, horses and swords, for with these am I in harmony
and find my pleasure in assaults and combats, liberality and
love-making."]

(A further source of his ideals is to be found in the *sirventes* "Volontiers fera
sirventes"—Gourian, no. 30, pp. 618–20, particularly stanzas IV and V.)

Love, war, poetry, liberality, singing, music, generous entertaining, courtesy which includes gallantry towards women: these are important elements in
this medieval world which Bertran embodies and symbolizes for Pound, a world
far removed from the respectable bourgeois world of twentieth century Wabash,
Philadelphia, or London. Nostalgia or utopia? In *Canto LXXX* (p. 543, Old
Edition), we have a passage beginning

But that New York I have found in Périgeux
　　si com' ad Arli
in wake of the saracen
　　　As the "surrender of Breda" (Velasquez)
was preceded in fresco at Avignon
　　　y cavals armatz with the perpendicular lances
and the red-bearded fellow was mending his
　　　young daughter's shoe
"Me Hercule! c'est notre commune"
('Borr', not precisely Altaforte)
　　　with such dignity

The description of the horses in the fresco at Avignon, rendered in Provençal,
a Provençal that takes us to the heart of this famous *canso* by de Born, then
leads naturally, by an easy association of ideas, to the peasant who seems still
to incarnate some of the dignity Pound takes to have been characteristic of a
previous way of life. This *sirventes*, with its praise of war and the whole ethos
of individual courageous heroic action, is also an important source for "Sestina:
Altaforte." (Another is lines 17–24 of "Ges de far sirventes no-m tartz," Gourian, Nol. 18, p. 352.) Furthermore, it ends with another favorite Poundian
formula:

Baron, metetz en gatge
Castels e vilas e ciutatz
Enans q'usqecs no-us gerraitz.

Pound's whole mythologizing of the Middle Ages, and in particular the manner
in which he envisaged Provence and the special place of the troubadours, above
all Bertran de Born, seems worthy of yet further speculation. Bertran is a factive
personality—a baron, a warrior, a counselor and companion of kings and princes,
a lover, a great poet—is he not Pound's ideal image of himself? More than one
person has, I believe, commented on the description of Bertran and how it can
appear to be a self-portrait; since none of the *vidas* or *rasos* provide us with any
description of En Bertrans, nor are there any pictures of him, Pound is free to
imagine him as he wishes:

a lean man? Bilious?
With a red straggling beard?
And the green cat's eyes lifts towards Montaignac.

Is Pound one of the many disappointed intellectuals of the twentieth
century who find in war and politics—a politics devoid of debate and doubt—in
a pre-industrial, pre-democratic, pre-capitalist world, their utopia, their dream
of a past yet to become the future? Is Pound's mythologizing of the troubadours,
what he deems to have been their world and its virtues and its dominant personal-
ities, one of the sources of his later political aberrations? What an unfair fate
for a fine poetical tradition that elevates "fin amor" and enshrines courtesy,
largesse, generosity, politeness, and distinguished manners as the hallmarks of
a truly civilized society of men and women! But all ages are full of contradic-
tions, and certainly in Bertran Pound could find elements of that peculiar aberra-
tion of twentieth century intellectuals which elevates force and violence to
supreme virtues.

NOTES

1. Stanislaw Stronski, *La légende amoureuse de Bertran de Born*, (Paris, 1914), cited by J. Bouti& A.H. Schutz, *Biographies des Troubadours*, second edition, (Paris, 1973), p. 74, note 1.

2. *L'Amour et la Guerre: L'Oeuvre de Bertran de Born* (Aix-en-Provence, 1985), p. 70.

3. For a fuller discussion of this problem, see Peter Makin, *Provence and Pound*, California, 1978, although Makin does not mention Gourian as his book appeared before the latter's edition.

4. In ''La civilization de l'Aquitaine à la fin de la période ducale,'' *Histoire de l'Europe Occidentale XIXIVSi*, Vol. II, Sec. IV, p. 27.

5. Hamlin, et al., p. 112, note ll. 33–36, and also see Rita Lejeune.

6. *The Companion to the Cantos*, Vol. I, p. 26.

7. See Klara Hallmeyer, *Bernart de Ventadour*, p. 75.

6

PETER MAKIN
Myth and *Hagoromo*

1. Why this nymph

I think one of the qualities that interested Pound in the *Hagoromo* myth was precision, and the point matters about *myth*, because there are ways of reading precision *out of* myths. It also matters about myth and *nature*, because a nature-myth is dependent on knowledge of nature. Nature is not just a word. Do Pound's myths really make us see anything of nature? If not, what can they tell us about anything else?

She whom Pound calls "the nymph of the *Hagoromo*" is connected quite tightly with a lot of things in the later Cantos: with the moon, with Fortuna, with Diana, with Venus, with Leucothea, and with some of the beings that circle delightedly round Dante as he rises through the spheres.[1] But what is the story doing in this passage?:

> and the later Beethoven on the new Bechstein,
> or in the Piazza S. Marco for example
> finds a certain concordance of size
>   not in the concert hall;
> can that be the papal major sweatin' it out to the bumm drum?
> what castrum romanum, what
>   "went into winter quarters"
> is under us?
> as the young horse whinnies against the tubas
>   in contending for certain values
> (Janequin per esempio, and Orazio Vecchii or Bronzino)
> Greek rascality against Hagoromo
>   Kumasaka vs. vulgarity
>   no sooner out of Troas
> than the damn fools attacked Ismarus of the Cicones
>   (*Canto LXXIX* p. 485)[2]

The ethic of these "damn fools," that is, Odysseus and his companions, was mere adventurism, and rightly punished; as such, perhaps typical of Western ethics, on which you could not build a durable empire; contrast Japanese ethics, as in the *Hagoromo*, based on self-knowledge and mutual responsibility. This is one of the things Pound was saying before and after Pearl Harbor.[3] But I would say the main point of Pound's whole quasi-epic poem is to establish a relation between politics and *aesthetics*. "Certain values": that is, aesthetic values: "Janequin per esempio." The young horse whinnies, thus contending for these values: its sound will be sharp, clear-edged. The opponents are the tubas, harrumph, the bumm drum, par*dum*, with the papal major *sweating* it out (thickness, fatness, mere gross effort), and the later Beethoven, whose grandness requires as its frame no mere concert hall but the Piazza San Marco (which so appealed to Napoleon as a super-salon), or an electric piano; all fitting with the simple-minded expansionism of the first Caesar who so efficiently trisected Gaul in his mind and brought the watercloset to farthest Britain. Such are the connections of this passage; and they lead to the political point thus: the Bechstein piano and Beethoven and the bumm drum lead to lies and to Greek rascality, lead thus to that tradition in the West that has so admired the brilliant con-trick, the wooden nutmeg-maker,[4] and (Pound's chief concern) the stock-market player who conjures a fortune out of nothing. The young horse and Janequin lead to *Hagoromo*, and honesty.

If one wants further proof that these alignments are in Pound's mind, one has only to follow up the reappearances of that military drum: it comes up as the usurer's pied-piper-of-Hamelin lure, the lure by which ignorant young men are set 'Knecht gegen Knecht' to slaughter each other by the thousand.[5]

Is this a valid chain of connection? Delicate clear music, as in Janequin, leads to beneficent politics? Pound's favouring of the light, the clear-edged, has been considered an arbitrary privileging of certain values, foisted on the reader by the usual sleights of authorial authority. But if we consider that the clear line, the thin line, is a line capable of fine detail, whereas a thick line is not, then it follows that Janequin's musical line can reflect the sound of birds by *exact placing*, where a fatter line would be merely a vague adumbration of it. One cannot be honest to complicated experience in a crude language.[6] The nymph of the *Hagoromo* is in this chain because she is honest. That is obvious. But if that is all she is, it seems too easy. She is innocent, and so forth: whatever "innocent" means. In the hands of critics often, and of Henry James at times, it seems ambiguously to mean both that she is prepubertal in sexuality, and that she has not yet collided with the nastiness of human nature. But Pound would have said there was no significant connection between those two.[7] I think there is something deeper in Pound's introduction of the *Hagoromo* nymph here; it is the connection between abundance and precision.

The nymph is, as it were, a free spirit. She has full use of the medium and resources she needs, chiefly the sky; she is not on the defensive; she is not calculating her advantage in a scarcity economics; so she has no need to hide, to blur, to falsify. If we realize that we too are in an abundance, we shall realize that we too have no need to falsify.

The *Hagoromo* nymph, then, is used for a lecture on honesty, which is precision. But she has to be an example of precision, or the lecture is mere words, and the mouthpiece could be anyone.

But precision about what? She has to be a precisely-seen *something*.

In the play, she allies honesty with freedom, coming from lack of dread. She embodies this freedom by being, in some sort, a creature of the air: in the original play, more a bird; in Pound's *Cantos*, more an inhabitant of the clouds. Then Pound has to persuade us that she is such a creature. He has to make us see her.

That, in my view, is how a myth works. The nymph has to *be* a bit of nature, and not any old bit, but this particular bit: girl and bird, or at least creature of the cloud-ways. I cannot emphasize too much that there is no other way of getting the necessary meaning into her.

But if Pound is permitted the resources of allusion in his Cantos, then the name *Hagoromo* itself should call forth what he wants: this creature of the air; *if* the play makes her so. Let us see if and how it does.[8]

2. Birds and ethics

The plot itself of the play makes the cloud-paths the focus, because its tension depends on them: they are what the girl has had cut off from her, and the plot is not resolved until they are restored. The whole to-and-fro of the first part, which is a tension of attitudes, depends on this need. This strongly colors the fact that she is a nymph of the moon; which is made prominent *later* than the *agon* establishing her relation with the birds and clouds.

From the moment the fisherman tells us he has found the robe and is taking it home, the disputation starts, and every step is material. The heavenly nymph, the *tennin*, has a very human sense of her difference: "That is a *tennin*'s robe and can't be so easily given to mere mortals";[9] and then, not "Give it back to me," but (more of a rebuke to the fisherman), "Put it back where it was," *Moto no gotoku ni oki tamae.* The fisherman does not then reply to that demand, but to the information contained in it: "Aha! then you must be a heavenly person." And there is fine comedy in his shift from the very deliberate way of thinking this out—"Then I'll make this a treasure for our earth here below"—to the super-blunt announcement of his conclusion: "No possibility of returning it." *Koromo o kaesu koto arumaji.* She protests, with a most desolate statement of what this will mean for her. And then we may *hear* him pumping up his resolve to be unpleasant—describing himself into an inhumanity: "The more I hear these words, the more mind-power I gain: from the beginning, I have been a

heartless person.'' And picking up the cloak and putting it behind him: *Kanomaji*.
''There is no possibility.''

The deed has been done, the tension of the plot has been established.
But we have only heard the nymph say ''Without that cloak the sky-ways wither
up for me, I cannot go back to the heavens.'' Neither the audience nor the
fisherman has yet been made to understand the extent of this disaster. Now there
begins one of those (to me) quite remarkable and affective musical-structural-
dramatic devices found from time to time in Noh plays, which so far as I can
discover has no formal name. It consists of a *mondo* or *kakeai*, a prose dialogue,
that diminishes into ever shorter sentences, then resolves into sung lyric statement by chorus and protagonist:[10]

> SHITE: Then now, though a *tennin*, like a wingless bird. If I
>   try to rise to the sky there is no cloak;
> WAKI: Living on this earth it becomes the lower world.
> SHITE: Trying this way, trying that way, though it is pitiful,
> WAKI: Because Hakuryo (the fisherman) does not return
>   the cloak,
> SHITE: Strength is insufficient,
> WAKI: There is nothing to be done.

Now follows the first resolution:

> CHORUS: Strings of beads of the dewdrops of her tears: the
> flowers of her hair-decoration wither, the five weakenings of
> the heavenly being can be seen before one's eyes, it is pitiful.
> SHITE: When I look back at the fields of heaven the mist is
> rising; I am lost in the cloud-paths, I do not know the direction
> to go.

—and the second resolution:

> CHORUS: Sooner or later the clouds will reach that part of
> heaven where you lived long and which you know well; how
> enviable their view. The voice of the phoenix which I am
> accustomed to becomes more faint; when I listen to the heaven-
> paths the geese are travelling home on, it fills me with longing;
> the plovers and the seagulls in the waves of the offing coming
> and going, and even the spring wind, fill me with longing.

I call this device ''a musical form'' because this particular shape (which
is an interaction between plot-shape; character; poetry; verbal rhythm; melody

and sung rhythm; and rhythm of instrumental accompaniment) has a formal ordered-ness that appears to be in itself affective, in the same way that sonnet-form is, or that sonata form is.

It also happens to be, as I have said, a recurrent sequence in Noh metrical forms and their accompaniment.[11] The shortening of the prose dialogue builds pace, and therefore tension, drawing into the impact and resolution of the first two lyric sections. In this case these lyric sections have a doubly resolving movement of their own. The first two are sung by different speakers, and in different kinds of verse-music: *ageuta* and *sageuta*; this is then resolved by strong lyric statement in which *one* speaker uses *both* kinds of verse-music in sequence, as it were the "A" and "B" motifs of sonata-form unified by being restated both in the home key.

"As in all great art," I am tempted to say, the structure is only made affective (is only made an emotive structure at all) by plot. As generally in this particular sequence in Noh, the prose dialogue is part of a struggle, a contention, between two voices, over an issue that has emotive power in the play.[12] It has to be a contention, or there is (putting it in musical terms) nothing to be "resolved" by the following song-sections as I have described them. But meanwhile this focusses attention on, and heightens, the dramatic conflict: also pointing towards a way out.

And here surfaces a peculiar feature that I think Pound certainly "took on board" in some part of his mind, though he never mentioned it (to my knowledge) in relation to *this* play. In 1934, the Noh scholar Chikara Igarashi published an article in which he pointed out that the allocation of speeches in the prose dialogue here is wrong. The end of the dialogue, we recall, went:

> SHITE: If I try to rise, there is no cloak;
> WAKI: Living on the earth it becomes the low world.
> SHITE: Trying this way, trying that way, though it is pitiful,
> WAKI: Because Hakuryo [the fisherman] does not return
>   the robe,
> SHITE: Strength is insufficient,
> WAKI: There is nothing to be done.

There is no reason for the fisherman to be speaking *any* of those lines; they all express feelings that, to judge by the interchange so far, would belong to the nymph. Yasuda, in his recent commentary, seems to think this oddity is unique to *Hagoromo*; but I noted it in at least two other plays before I came across Igarashi's observation of it here, and think it would probably have struck scholars earlier if it had not been for a certain reverence that enshrines Noh poetry.[13] What it might suggest to an audience is that the fisherman is already inside the maiden's feelings more than he is inside his own; that his flinty short-sightedness is already changing.

That the Noh could express such a change by an interchange of voices is only in common with its whole armoury of techniques to convey what I would call "the migration of consciousness"; and I think that that is the content that Pound was more interested in than any other in his dealings with the Noh. It is what, more than anything else, he tried to imitate in his own Noh play, only recently published, *Tristan*.[14]

All this shaping, in the present passage, places a great weight on the lyric passages at the end of it; whose function is to tell us precisely what the maiden has lost.

"When I look *back* at the fields of heaven," she says: *Ama no hara,/ furisakemireba* . . . : in one of those strangely suggestive multiple compounds that appear sometimes in the Noh. She says "fields of heaven": though such phrases are as "fixed" as any in *Beowulf* or Homer, this does not diminish their power: the tradition fixed them because of their power. What she envies is *what the clouds see* there:[15] they are living inhabitants of the upper sky that, till now, was also hers.

"When I *listen to the heaven-paths* the geese are travelling home on": she listens to the space, the place of movement, the movement of the birds who have a direction and for whom the heaven-roads are part of their power to answer their longings by movement.

All that fills her with longing is movement, even the plovers and seagulls in the lower sky, "coming and going" with the spring wind.

All this is a main part of the objective correlative that the Noh play (and hence also Pound) are creating: a longing for a lost power of untrammelled ascent, which is the most emotive form of the power of movement itself. This lost freedom is the basis of the distress at what has happened. And the sense of what has been lost is tied by that dramatic moment—a moment of *doubt*, in a proceeding action—to the main psychological complex that it is set against, the fisherman's calculatingness, because the doubt-tension is resolved as soon as he abandons that.

And so I think Pound was quite right to take it that this exchange with the fisherman was not just a piece of pastoral comedy, a *captatio benevolentiae* for the serious business of celebrating spring that follows; *or* an easy allegory for easy truths we know anyway—"fallen man is not pure," or "pure man is not fallen"[16]; but a fulcrum of psychic realities strong enough to set against the ethics of Odysseus and of creative finance.

And it is clear that the whole depends on the concrete—"poetic"—establishing of the girl's relations with the sky.

With the establishing of those relations, the heaven-girl may be said to enter the company of all those power-creatures that have worn wings since remote ages: the Babylonian bull-birds or *Karibu* that were the ancestors of Ezekiel's *cherubim*,[17] and hence of St. John's angels and hence of Dante's; the shamans who fly as birds in bird-cloaks in present-day Siberia, and whom Pound seems to suggest when he tells his reader to imagine the nymph's headdress by looking at the "examples of state head-dress of kingfisher feathers in the South Kensington Museum"[18]; Pound himself identifying with the "king-wings," the great butterflies that in their fragility cross the gulf to the temple[19]; and the mind of the contemplator as Richard of St. Victor tells us we should imagine it: "birds for the mind," *in avibus intellige studia spiritualia.*[20] It seems that when Zeami constructed *Hagoromo*, and some five other plays, he took the form of the *tennyo-mai*, the heavenly maiden's dance, from his illustrious predecessor Doami; and he records that Doami "danced the heavenly maiden, lightly and quickly, just like a bird drifting at the mercy of the wind."[21]

And it might be that we should think of the 'birdliness' of these birds as more important than any particular theological or doctrinal tradition they are embedded in. When, in the *Pisan Cantos*, Pound has the *Hagoromo* nymph coming to him "as a corona of angels," he is calling on a visual tradition of winged persons so powerful that it overcomes the context in Dante that he is thinking of. For Dante is not thinking of angels when he says

> Io vidi più fulgór vivi e vincenti
> Far di noi centro e di sē far corona[22]

and Dante's angels in the *Paradiso* scarcely have wings. In this area, imagination (or the need of such identifications) has always overcome theology; theology has been moulded by a string of *fantastica* and apocrypha, from St. John the Divine to Dionysius the Areopagite. So that when Fra Angelico grows wings so finely and exactly out of Gabriel, he is doing something quite as "primitive" as a Siberian shaman wearing his bird-cloak; his complex image is not the less myth because it is official.

These seem to me some of the "affects" Pound was drawing on, closely or remotely, by invoking the *Hagoromo*.

3. Folcloristica

If Pound found that the nymph defined something with precision, I think he discovered it by reading the notes that Hirata dictated to Fenollosa, in some such manner as I have just read the play.[23] For Pound (though later he read too much and too thinly) in his heyday had an unsurpassed ability to read works of literature as shapes (structures); and this it was that, among other things, made him the most effective working editor of contemporary literature that the English-speaking world has known. But I should like to consider another way of finding meaning in the play: by reading it as a piece of folklore.

The story of the celestial maiden seems to have been taken by Zeami, the supposed author of *Hagoromo*, from some lost version of a common folktale. Versions of this tale still circulate in rural Japan.[24] An ancient example of it can be found in the *Fudoki* (eighth century) from the old region of Tango, close to where I now live. The story says that an old couple saw eight heavenly maidens bathing, so they stole the mantle belonging to one of them. When the others flew off, she was left to beg for the return of her cloak. The old man accused her of trying to trick them; she replied, in effect, "Doubt is for mortals." She went to live with them. She made a divine liquor, by which the old couple eventually got rich. Then they told her to go away. She wept, and said "I have been reduced to this earthly world and have lost the way to heaven." She sang, "Looking up at the sky in the distance,/A haze hides the way to heaven,/I do not know where to go." She wandered off to various villages, and finally became a local goddess at Nagu no Yashiro.[25]

Folklorists will readily see here a form of the 'Swan-Maiden' story; variants are scattered from Scandinavia to Persia to Alaska, from the third century A.D. to now.[26] Uno Harva gives an example from the Buryats of modern Siberia:

> Once upon a time, three swans came down to a lake to swim. When they had taken off their bird-costumes, they changed into splendid women. A hunter called Khoredoj, who had hidden on the bank, stole one of the garments and hid it. When the women-swans had swum for a while, they came out of the water to dress; but the one whose garment had disappeared stayed naked on the shore, while the others flew off. The hunter took the woman and married her. As the years passed, she gave birth to eleven sons and six daughters. One day she remembered her former garment and asked her husband where he had hidden it; he, certain that his wife could not abandon him or her children, decided to return to her this wonderful garment. The woman put it on to see what she would look like; but as soon as she had done so, she flew up through the chimney-hole. Gliding above the house, she cried to those she had abandoned: "You are terrestrial beings and will stay on earth, but I am from the sky and am going back there." As she rose up, she said: "Every spring, when the swans fly towards the north, and every autumn, when they come back, you must perform special ceremonies in my honor!" Then she disappeared into the heavens. The Buryats add that one of her daughters, whose hands were dirty with soot, tried to stop her mother from flying off by grabbing her feet; wherefore the feet of the swan are black.[27]

Harva was the first to note the close resemblance between this story and that found in an eighth-century Chinese source; which Chinese source may well be an ancestor of the Japanese story that Zeami had in mind when he wrote *Hagoromo*.[28] Harva observed that among the Siberian Buryats the story appeared to be an example of totemism in the strict sense: the belief that a family was descended from a certain animal. But also, Harva observed that such animals were held to act as assistants to the shamans of the tribes in these regions. A Buryat shaman sings: "A grey hare is our courier, a grey wolf our messenger, the swan is our transformer, the eagle is our envoy."[29]

In 1980, A.T. Hatto published a survey of swan-maiden stories, stripped down to their essentials, and noted that they come largely from "the region in which the classic forms of shamanism occur." The shaman very commonly has bird-motifs in his magic cloak; and Hatto says (quoting Ohlmarks), "It appears that the idea of the shaman's spirit-journey through the air in a manner resembling the flight of birds is at the bottom of the so-called 'Bird-Type' of Asiatic shaman's cloak." The shaman's spirit, on its journey, commonly rises through the roof-vent, like the bird-woman in the Buryat story. And "in archaic society 'foreign women' (of whom bird-women are the quintessential type) are regularly suspected of sorcery . . . "

This is significant for Hatto's thesis, for he regards the swan-maiden story as a representation of two things. First,

> At the human level the story has to do with the pitiable lot of a girl from another tribe who has been trapped into an unsuitable union through the guile and strength of a man. So much does it tell the woman's side of the story—whether sympathetically from within or scathingly from without (at the expense of the "foreign woman")—that one suspects its first tellers may have been women.[30]

Secondly, the story comes geographically from the areas of North Asia where the great migratory water-birds mate. In spring, they fly north to mate and rear their offspring; in autumn, they fly south. As autumn approaches. There is in some species . . . a time when both the young (because they are not fully fledged) and the parents (because they are in moult) cannot fly, so that the change in mood when they can is dramatic. Man once had to tame his ducks and swans and geese, and so there was a time when he was able to observe how intensely the urge to fly away in autumn assailed his half-wild birds—all the more so if he had taken the precaution of cutting their wing-feathers. At this level, then, the story deals with birds of passage.[31]

Now I, having correlated these data from the *Fudoki*, from the *Taketori monogatari*, from the modern *mukashi-banashi* or folk-tales, from Waley, from

Sieffert, from Seki, from Levy, from Harva, from Hatto and from Ginzburg, am under a great temptation to brandish a shamanistic interpretation as the meaning of the *Hagoromo* story in Pound's *Cantos*. For Pound's poem places this sky-nymph with a group of female interveners, of rescuers, of imparters of an unlooked-for and inexplicable "grace" which frees the Odysseus-protagonist (in the later *Cantos*) from the tangles of his own rationalist and will-manufactured despair. Leucothea says "my bikini is worth your raft"[32]: that is, "Give up the apparatus that your reason so reasonably tells you must hang on to; give yourself up to my unpredictable and divine goodwill." The chief point about this "grace" is that it comes from outside, that is, it is nothing that the hero could have excogitated for himself; it is inexplicable. Its imparters are always female; and his relation with them is always to a certain degree sexual ("and the greatest is charity/ to be found among those who have not observed/ regulations" (*Canto LXXIV*, p. 434) clearly fits with Pound's view of that second Venus, Cunizza[33]). And do we not find that in the swan-maiden stories the swan-girl herself is the earthling's lover, while in shamanistic cults the spirit-swan can be the shaman's lover? A. T. Hatto says:

> Another shamanistic conception which may be linked with the Swan Maiden story is one according to which, to quote Dr. Waley, "the shaman's relation with the Spirit is represented as a kind of love-affair." Dr. Waley also refers to this relationship as a "mantic honeymoon." The shaman may be either a man or a woman, and the Spirit is always of the opposite sex . . . Emerging from his trance, the shaman (like certain European mystics) feels as though abandoned by his or her Spirit-lover, who ascends to Heaven, sometimes from a mythical mountain.[34]

Q.E.D., we should read the *Hagoromo* nymph in the *Cantos* as the embodiment of a shaman's (Pound's) guiding animal-spirit.

But I should like to argue that this is no particularly useful way to the meaning of the *Hagoromo* nymph, whether in the play or in Pound's poem, at all.

4. Against mythography

To me, Hatto's conclusions about the migratory birds are very attractive. But what is the shape of his argument? On the one hand, he progressively strips details from the variants of the swan-maiden stories, in an attempt to find the formula that is the centre. (Again and again we find formulae like " 'its irreducible gist,' " "the essential plot.' "[35]) This is a movement towards generality, that is, towards the deep vagueness of motif-juggling, where one story can be classified differently from another because it includes, or does not include, a dog. On the other hand, Hatto progressively adds details to this picture of migratory water-fowl, till his description of them becomes, as one might say, "poetic."

The description of the birds is as full and as concrete as one could wish. But it is necessarily a minuscule band of the huge spectrum of experience that life for the Buryats or Tungus or Dolgans must necessarily consist of. Meanwhile the only reason given by the mythographer for selecting those particular tribes to draw experience from is that the bits of selected experience themselves are held to have an affinity with the swan-maiden stories. And that depends on his reading of the stories.

It is no different from the method of that great late-Romantic tourist of the senses, Walter Pater. He had been to the Mediterranean lands; he had seen the grapes on their hot hillsides; and by God he could write prose-poems fit to convince anyone of the relevance of that baked earth to the myth of Dionysus.[36] What tells us that his rhapsodies convey what was in the minds of Greeks when they thought of grapes and of Dionysus? Only the selection of data and their shaping in the rhapsodies themselves. But I submit that this is the basic method of myth-readers. It betrays itself every time a Carlo Ginzburg says some conjecture is "undoubtedly alien to the spirit of the myth," or "patently absurd."[37]

In any case, supposing the feelings of migratory water-fowl to be relevant to the interpretation of swan-maiden stories, one would have to be blind to birds not to have had such feelings oneself, concerning their desires to move, to fly. Why do we need to know that the Tungus have them? And without such feelings, the proposing of origins among tribes who see those birds does nothing to explain the continued effect.[38] One identified oneself with birds before knowing that the Tungus identified themselves with them; or that their shamans drew powers from them; or indeed what a shaman was.

The new data brought by a Hatto, then, are as "neutral" in value, and as dispensable, as the new data brought by a Pater. But I should like to point out the disastrous effects of the *loss* of data caused by the other element of this method, which is a process of boiling stories down to find the "essential" elements, the "motifs." It seems not to be noticed that this is in fact the second boiling-down: the first occurs when the story is taken out of its original language and its original shapes of presentation.

It seems to me that such a loss occurs also in all structuralist-formalist readings of myth, and perhaps in all readings of myth as myth.

For example, I would not be the first to point out that in Lévi-Strauss the relation between what I shall call (B), the discerned elements of folktales, and what I shall call (C), the binary oppositions that the mythographer sorts them into, is essentially arbitrary: that the plot-elements could most often be described and divided in a different way, and the results allocated quite otherwise.[39] But it seems to me too often forgotten that (B) is already the result of a stripping, a denudation that arbitrarily selects meaning: that there is a stage (A) in which these stories existed before the mythographers re-presented them to us. That is, they existed *in* a given language, which the mythographer very often cannot read (Lévi-Strauss could not read Bororo), and *in* a set of inner shapes ("artistic structures") where are not decorators but makers of meaning. Sequence (and non-sequence) of thought; shift of diction; image-echo and image-quality: all these modify the meanings of object and of action.

True, the mythographer often professes to consider myth-elements within a structure; but one finds all he means is structures (of narrative, of contrast, etc.) constituted by the story-elements *as already denuded and re-shaped by him*; that is, in his or some other mythographer's summary.

And if it be said that most folktales do not have the complex kind of shaping that I have been talking about, the kind we find in *Hagoromo*: I answer that, to judge by their published lucubrations, mythographers are not commonly in a position to know whether they have such shaping or not. The currency of mythographers is summaries.

The nymph of the *Hagoromo* and Dante's angels indeed converge; but they converge by virtue of the power of the shapings that they are imbedded in, and that create the precise direction of their meanings. Which shapings do not survive summary and atomisation, standard first steps in the mythographer's method.

Pound did well to be largely innocent of the reading of any of his literature as myth-carriers: as variant surfaces to be compared, in order to find logically preexistent "essential stories." He did well to read them, instead, with the tremendous sympathetic capacity of his intelligence, as interlocked shapings of verbal indicators of experience, or what is called "art."*

*(I should like to acknowledge the generous help of Professor Nobuyuki Yuasa, who first guided me through Noh texts; Professor Akira Yasukawa, Professor Tetsuhiko Kamimura and Mr. Genjiro Okura of the Okura School of *kotsuzumi* players, who advised me on language and backgrounds; John L. Makin, who found essential texts; Mr. Yoshimitsu Nayakama and Mr. Haruki Lee, who helped with translations; and Ms. Miki Ishihara, who gave expert advice.)

NOTES

NOTE: Abbreviations for titles of texts by Pound are as those used in the *Companion to the Cantos of Ezra Pound*, ed. Carroll F. Terrell, Berkeley and Los Angeles: University of California Press, 1980–84.

1. *Hagoromo* is referred to at 74/430, 79/487, 80/500, and 106/755. The later Cantos closely associate the moon with Fortuna; 'plenilune,' the tag for the moon-as-Fortuna at 97/679, is from *Paradiso* 23.25, with which Pound particularly compares the *Hagoromo* moon-nymphs in *T*, p. 313. The nymph-protagonist of *Hagoromo* is brought to mind by clouds as well as moon at 80/500; the movement of the clouds across the sky then evokes that of Venus in her Botticellian *nautile*, and of Olga coming ashore in a sunset lit the colour of copper (Venus' colour) (cf. Massimo Bacigalupo, *L'Ultimo Pound*, Rome: Edizioni di Storia e Letteratura, 1981, pp. 152–58.) For Leucothea, note that the *Hagoromo* nymph is 'immacolata' at 80/500, and cf. 80/513, 'when the raft broke and the waters went over me,/Immaculata, Introibo.' For the beings that circle round Dante during his ascent, cf. 74/430 ('and the nymph of the Hagoromo came to me,/as a cona of angels') with *Paradiso* 10.64–65.

2. In what follows, Cantos passages are quoted in the text of the Faber 'Revised Collected' edition of 1975. On the themes of this passage, see also Peter Makin, *Pound's Cantos*, repr. Baltimore: Johns Hopkins University Press, 1992, pp. 242–245.

3. On Odysseus' trickery see esp. 80/512 ('the folly of attacking that island'), with which cf. *LE* p. 212 and *CON* p. 23; on the values implicit in the Noh plays see esp. 74/442 and *"Ezra Pound Speaking": Radio Speeches of World War II*, ed. Leonard W. Doob, Westport, Conn.: Greenwood Press, 1978, p. 385.

4. See *SP* p. 171.

5. 74/428, 76/462–3, 79/487; the "bumm drum" clearly derives from FitzGerald's version of Omar Khayyam, read by Pound in the detention centre at Pisa in Speare's *Pocket Book of Verse* (cf. Makin, *Pound's Cantos*, pp. 243, 251).

6. See especially *GK* pp. 281–2 on 'discrimination by the senses', and avarice.

7. The quasi-identification of the *Hagoromo* nymph with Venus at 80/500 (see above Note 1) would be curious if one took the nymph to be 'immacolata' in the sense of 'virginal.'

8. On the relation between Ernest Fenollosa, his teacher Eiichi Hirata, and the notes that Pound used, see the essential article by Scott Johnson, ''The Fenollosa-Hirata Manuscripts on Noh and How Pound Edited Them,'' in *Transactions of the Conference of Orientalists in Japan,* 23 (1978) pp. 49–59. In what follows I shall be discussing the Japanese text of *Hagoromo*, which Pound of course did not see; for a justification of this procedure see below, note 23.

9. Translations in what follows are mine, based on *Yokyokushu* ed. Hiroshi Koyama et al. (Nihon Koten Bungaku Zenshu), Tokyo: Shogakkan, 1973–75, Vol. 1 pp. 351–60.

10. Prose conversations are called *kakeai*, but there is no special name for the shape that arises when the alternation of speakers creates an intensity, which is heightened as the lines shorten and achieves a climax and resolution when the statement of both interlocutors is taken over by the Chorus.

11. The shape may be found in *Sotoba Komachi* (*Yokyokushu*, ed. cit., Vol. 2 pp. 77–78); in *Kumasaka* (op. cit., Vol. 2 pp. 375–76); in *Tadanori* (op. cit., Vol. 1 pp. 160–61), etc.

12. In the case of *Sotaba Komachi*, the contention is over the shallow view of religious proprieties taken by the two priests. Komachi's ghost overturns this view and simultaneously shows that she is not the bumpkin she was mistaken for. In *Tadanori*, the contention is merely between literary sensibilities, with (again) the function of revealing that Tadanori's ghost is not the ordinary fisherman he was condescendingly taken to be.

13. See the citation of Igarashi in Kenneth Yasuda, ed., *Masterworks of the No Theater*, Bloomington: Indiana University Press, 1989, pp. 140, 145–46, and 526 note 58. In *Kumasaka* and *Sotoba Komachi*, this exchange of consciousnesses occurs as part of the particular musical shape I have been discussing. In *Sotoba Komachi* it may merely represent the persuasion of the priests by Komachi; but in *Kumasaka* there is no such explanation, for the priest interrogates Kumasaka using information that, logically, he cannot know. In *Kayoi Komachi* (*Yokyokushu*, ed. cit., Vol. 2 pp. 158–59), and in other cases, there are 'mergings of consciousness' that do not coincide with the musical shape I have been describing.

14. *Plays Modelled on the Noh (1916)*, ed. Donald C. Gallup, Toledo: Friends of the University of Toledo Libraries, 1987, pp. 31–38. The play concerns the mutual psychic dependence of the ghosts of Tristan and Yseult, who "flash and fade through each other," and speak through the voice of the Sculptor who has encountered them, as they struggle to re-attain full existence.

15. "Sooner or later the clouds will reach that part of heaven . . . How enviable their view."

16. See e.g. *No et Kyogen: Printemps, Été*, ed. René Sieffert, Paris: Publications Orientalistes de France, 1979, p. 90: *Hagoromo* "n'est rien d'autre qu'un long poème chantant la nature printanière."

17. See e.g. Denys l'Aréopagite, *La Hiérachie Céleste*, ed. René Roques, Paris: Éditions du Cerf, 1970, p. 104 note.

18. *T* p. 310 note.

19. 106/754, cf. 92/619 etc.

20. 90/607; cf. Pound, tr., 'Selections from Richard of St. Victor' in *Gnomon* 2 (Spring 1967) p. 36.

21. *Zeami's Talks on Sarugaku: An Annotated Translation of the Sarugaku Dangi*, ed. Erika de Poorter, Amsterdam: J.C. Gieben, 1986, p. 83.

22. 74/430; *Paradiso* 10.64–65.

23. Most of the structures that I have been describing survive into a full prose translation such as Pound had in the Fenollosa notes. Pound knew no Japanese, and much has been made of the misunderstandings of the Fenollosa material to which he was thus subject (see e.g. Nobuko Tsukui, *Ezra Pound and Japanese Noh Plays*, Washington, D.C.: University Press of America, 1983, *passim*). But it seems to me that the mistakes are mostly of quite trivial effect, in comparison with the semantic richness made available to Pound by the form Fenollosa imposed on his notes. This form consisted of two or even three levels of literality for each sentence, of which (it has been observed by Akiko Miyake) Pound always preferred to follow the word-for-word. This practice brought him far closer than would any ordinary paraphrase to the experience-splittings, concept-juxtaposings and concept-orderings inherent in the original Japanese. Where Pound was led astray

from the literal sense by this method, his errings are often genuinely creative, in the sense of filling out lines of thought and emotion implicit in the main structures that the surrounding data have allowed him to perceive. The unnoticed paradox is that Pound's results are, as a whole, more precise than those of Fenollosa, in the cases where Fenollosa produced finished translations of whole passages; for Fenollosa's poetic English, like that of Emerson, is radically vague in its conceptualisations.

24. See Keigo Seki, ed., *Folktales of Japan*, Chicago: University of Chicago Press, 1963, pp. 63–69.

25. For the stories from Tango, Omi and Suruga, see *Fudoki*, ed. Yoshiro Aki-moto (Nihon Koten Bungaku Taikei), Tokyo: Iwanami, 1958, pp. 470–77, 457–60, 447–48. See also the 9th or 10th Century version in "Le Conte du Coupeur de Bambous" ed. René Sieffert, in *Bulletin de la Maison Franco-Japonaise*, n.s., 2 (1953), esp. pp. 123–35, 175–93.

26. See esp. A.T. Hatto, *Essays on Medieval German and Other Poetry*, Cambridge: Cambridge University Press, 1980, pp. 267–68.

27. Uno Harva, *Les représentations religieuses des peuples altaïques*, Paris: Gallimard, pp. 318–19 (my translation).

28. Cf. Hatto, op. cit., pp. 269–272. Howard S. Levy, "Rainbow Skirt and Feather Jacket," in *Literature East and West* 13 (1969), pp. 132–4, 137, 111–25, and Arthur Waley, 'The Chinese Cinderella Story,' in *Folk-Lore* 58 (1947), p. 232.

29. Harva, op. cit., p. 324.

30. Hatto, op. cit., pp. 283, 286, 275.

31. Hatto, op. cit., p. 274.

32. 91/616.

33. See *Guide to Kulchur* pp. 107–08 and Peter Makin, *Provence and Pound*, Berkeley and Los Angeles: University of California Press, 1978, pp. 200–201.

34. Hatto, op. cit., p. 287. There seems to be a problem in the fact that this particular form of shamanism has not been found in the bird-migration areas.

35. Hatto, op. cit., pp. 272, 275.

36. Dionysus' fruition is the grape, Pater explains, which is light and fluid combined: the sun shrivels the earth, as Zeus shrivelled Semele in the conceiving of Dionysus, and the result is the fluid globe of the grape, whose freshness and translucence seem to contrast with the scorched Mediterranean earth around it. "He is *purigenes*, then, fire-born, the son of lightning, lightning being to light, as regards concentration, what wine is to the other strengths of the earth." (See Makin, *Pound's Cantos*, ed. cit., p. 97, and Walter Pater, *Greek Studies*, London: Macmillan, 1904, p. 26.)

37. *Ecstasies: Deciphering the Witches' Sabbath*, New York: Pantheon Books, 1991, p. 227, with reference to the Oedipus myth, which is connected by Ginzburg with Cinderella and hence with the swan-maiden stories.

38. Hatto's method is to be valued in so far as it adduces concrete data: thereby showing some consciousness of nature as it exists—outside the library—a thing conspicuously lacking in much literary criticism.

39. Claude Lévi-Strauss, *The Raw and the Cooked*, Chicago: University of Chicago Press, 1983, gives ready examples of barefaced wilfulness in filling out an ideal scheme where data are lacking (p. 137), arbitrary decisions as to when to interpret "literally" and when not (p. 148), predetermination that all experience should subserve binary antitheses (p. 153), and arbitrary attribution of data to one side or the other of these (passim). These weapons give the mythographer an insulation from experience (as embodied in myths), and a freedom in constructing schemes, unequalled, I think, since the cosmography of the High Middle Ages.

7

MICHAEL FAHERTY

The Myth of the Mad Celtic King:
Another Voice in the *Pisan Cantos*?

Ever since their publication in 1948, the *Pisan Cantos* have enjoyed a popularity often denied the rest of Pound's epic poem. Although some critics claim that they cannot be read by themselves—as a sort of mini-long poem—others insist that they stand up very well on their own, with some of Pound's best readers admitting that it was their initial enjoyment of the *Pisan Cantos* that decided them to go back and begin at *Canto 1*. As time passes and the years distance us from 1948 and the events surrounding the Second World War and Pound's internment at Pisa, it seems increasingly unlikely that readers turn to the *Pisan Cantos* again and again merely for their moments of lyric beauty or their tragic autobiographical and historical content. Rather, it would appear that their lasting appeal might be found in some underlying and unrecognized mythic structure, some highly elegiac story of worlds lost and worlds found.

Much of their appeal has been attributed to the mythic role-playing that takes place in these cantos, the chorus of *voices* that speak here, the aural memory that comes flooding back. But at the same time it has also been argued that the real excitement of the *Pisan Cantos* comes from the fact that it is here that Pound's *lyric* voice returns, it is here, in the *Pisan Cantos*, that Pound finally lets the mask slip a bit, or at least allows the reader to have a brief peek behind the mask. What I would like to suggest is that this *voice*, which has often been identified as Pound's own, might actually be yet another mask, one he borrowed from a fellow poet whose presence pervades these cantos.

I am speaking, of course, of Yeats. As has often been noted, it was Yeats, as much as Browning, who taught Pound how to use the mask in his poetry. However, it was not a lesson to be learned during the three Stone Cottage winters in Sussex but a technique he had mastered before he met Yeats for the first time in 1909. Much of Pound's early poetry, particularly those poems published in *A Lume Spento*, is saturated with the influence of Yeats. As James Longenbach has noted, this slim early volume is "filled with echoes of the poet he longed to meet."[1] Pound, of course, gives Yeats the proper bend of the knee in his Note Precedent to the poem "La Fraisne," originally intended to be the title poem of the collection. He informs the reader that the poem was written heavily under Yeats's influence, with the "mood" of his Celtic Twilight stories thoroughly in mind.[2] However, if one goes to these stories—which Yeats claims he mostly heard from one Paddy Flynn, who was usually to be found beside his peat fire eating mushrooms or sleeping beneath some hedge[3]—it is clear that it isn't these tales of the "little people" that Pound had in mind but rather the poetry itself, particularly the verse contained in volumes such as his 1895 *Poems*, *The Wind Among the Reeds*, and *In the Seven Woods*.

In his Note Precedent to "La Fraisne," Pound states that he found himself in a "mood" that has often been associated with the literature of the early Irish Renaissance, a feeling that there was a division between his "corporal" self and his "aetherial" self. To capture this, he wanted to tell the story of "a dweller by streams and in woodland." He explained:

> When the soul is exhausted by fire, then doth the spirit return
> unto its primal nature and there is upon it a peace great and
> of the woodland . . . Then becometh it kin to the faun and the
> dryad, a woodland-dweller amid the rocks and streams.[4]

Although Pound could have turned to several of Yeats's early poems for such a mask, the poem "La Fraisne" most closely resembles is one of Yeats' first poems, an 1884 poem written when he was only nineteen years old, "The Madness of King Goll." Both poems begin by informing the reader that the speakers once lived terribly regal lives, quite the opposite of their present conditions. In Yeats's poem, we are told that the speaker once "sat on cushioned otter-skin" and "mused and drank sweet wine"; his "word was law" throughout much of Ulster and should a herdsman come to him complaining that pirates had stolen his swine, he would summon soldiers "From rolling vale and rivery glen / And under the blinking of the stars" to pitch them into the sea from whence they came.[5] Likewise, the speaker in Pound's poem informs us that he was once "a gaunt, grave councillor / Being in all things wise" who in his day, he assures us more than once in the poem, "was quite strong—at least they said so—/ The young men at the sword-play" (*CEP* 9–10). However, both men have clearly left all this behind for a solitary life in the wild where they have become friend to plant and animal alike: Pound's figure having taken "a dogwood tree" and "a pool of the wood" for his bride, while the Mad King Goll has befriended the "grey wolf" and is able to lead the "woodland deer" along by tugging on his ear. In both poems, however, it is clear that the speakers have not found a wholly idyllic peace. King Goll admits that he "must wander wood and hill / Through summer's heat and winter's cold" and, in the final stanza, he utters a rather tragic lament, followed by the poem's refrain, which suggests that although the wilds are now his home, his life is anything but bliss: "They will not hush, the leaves a-flutter round me, the beech leaves old." As has been pointed out by other critics, this same line is echoed in Pound's poem. Just as the Mad King Goll has found that he can "quench" the "whirling and wandering fire'' in his head that originally sent him to the woods by playing upon a stolen tympan, the speaker in Pound's poem is counselled by nature, his ''bride,'' to keep madness at bay by ''Bidding me praise / Naught but the wind that flutters in the leaves.'' Both figures find that by turning to poetry and song they can fight the tears and at least temporarily ease the physical and mental anguish of their existence.

Even though Pound tells us in his Note Precedent to ''La Fraisne'' that the mask he has put on is not that of a Celtic King but of the troubadour Bisclavret (*CEP* 8)—whose story is not unlike that of Piere Vidal, ''the fool par excellence of all Provence'' who also ''ran mad, as a wolf,'' through the woods (109)—one would be hard put without Pound's instruction to see the poem as Provençal in any way. The ''still pool'' where the speaker finds himself is known as the double-hyphenated ''Mar-nan-otha,'' which Pound clearly intends to sound Celtic not unlike, for example, ''Clooth-na-Bare'' in another of Yeats's early poems which Pound often singled out for praise, ''Red Hanrahan's Song about Ireland'' (*YP* 133). Although Pound said in the Stone Cottage years that he had tired of the Celtic Twilight, it was always this sort of Yeats poem that Pound liked best: the poetry of the 1880s and the 1890s, full of mist and fog, lost wandering souls, and an occasional spirit or two. The ''King Goll'' poem—which the young Pound enjoyed enough to imitate—tells only one of many Celtic stories of the Mad and Fallen King. Although these stories are usually classified as part of one of the historical cycles of early Irish literature, the Cycle of Kings, they are also considered a sort of genre or sub-genre of their own. The smaller cycle from which the story of Goll comes is known as the Cycle of Domhnall, and within this cycle the most famous version of the tale is the story of the Mad King Sweeney. In fact, it is believed that the story of King Goll has been so contaminated by the better-known legend of King Sweeney that the two stories and the two figures can no longer be completely separated. The source which Yeats has given for his early knowledge of the legend, Eugene O'Curry's *Lectures on the Manuscript Materials of Ancient Irish History*, includes equal mention of both tales and, in our own century, the figure of Sweeney has completely overshadowed that of Goll. Not only did Flann O'Brien make him a figure of admiration as well as fun in his novel *At Swim-Two-Birds* (O'Brien includes a lengthy excerpt of the legend in his book and wanted to change the title to *Sweeney in the Trees* but the publishers refused) but, perhaps more famously in recent years, Seamus Heaney has published his own translation of the story in *Sweeney Astray*. Both Goll and Sweeney were East Ulster kings who, according to some accounts, fell in battle or who, according to others, went mad amidst the carnage and flew into the wilds—in Sweeney's case, quite literally.

The Sweeney legend is one of many famous legends and stories to have arisen following the Battle of Magh Rath in the year 637, one of the most decisive battles of early Irish history. In the story, Sweeney, King of Dal-Arie, runs afoul of the cleric St. Ronan Finn, who not only proposes to build a church within his kingdom, driving Sweeney mad with the ringing of his bell, but who, at the battle, accidentally sprinkles the pagan king with a few drops of holy water. Never known for his restraint or reserve, Sweeney spears one of St. Ronan's psalmists and launches a spear at the saint himself, cracking his bell. As a result, Ronan puts a curse on Sweeney, pronouncing that "He shall roam Ireland, mad and bare" and, what's more, that he shall do so in the manner of a bird[6]. As one of O'Brien's characters points out in *At Swim-Two-Birds*, "You won't get very far [in Ireland] by attacking the church."[7] The remainder of the text consists of Sweeney's wanderings throughout Ireland and Britain, resting here and there atop some tree, exposed to the wind and rain, and forced to survive on a diet of watercress and spring water. Like Goll, Sweeney's state of mind alternates between utter despair and exultation: despair when he thinks of what he has left behind—friends, family, his reputation and power, and all the comforts of life indoors—and exultation when he looks about him and realizes that although he may have lost one kingdom, he has gained another—that of the green world.

In the Irish legends, Sweeney is often referred to as a *geilt*, who were considered to be "inspired madmen," often associated with the bird-like charac-teristics and abilities that are used to describe the exiled figure of Sweeney. These so-called madmen were also known for their poetic abilities, whether the ability to pluck the strings of the tympan "with sound like falling dew," as in Goll's case, or an almost unsurpassed gift for nature lyrics, as in the case of Sweeney. In fact, it is the poetry that Sweeney left behind rather than the story itself that accounts for the legend's popularity over the centuries. Many promi-nent Celtic scholars consider it some of the finest nature poetry in all of Irish literature. As Heaney has pointed out, Sweeney has always been seen by Irish writers as "a figure of the artist, displaced, guilty, assuaging himself by his utterance."[8] It is clear from Yeats's use of King Goll that he also saw him as a figure of the poet, despite the fact that he preferred a stringed instrument to the voice. Perhaps Pound wanted to make this point even clearer by telling the reader that the mask he is using in "La Fraisne" is that of the mad troubadour who has turned his talents from the praise of "the love of women" to "the wind that flutters in the leaves."

The question, of course, is whether or not Pound had these figures in mind when composing the *Pisan Cantos*. Clearly, it is the memories of these early years and his study and friendship with Yeats that dominate these cantos. Would he then—finding himself in a situation remarkably like that of Goll and Sweeney, having lost his world in a war, exposed to the elements of wind and rain, separated from family and friends, sensing that his mind is slowly slipping out of his control, and turning to the green world and its celebration in poetry for moments of release from almost intolerable suffering—would he have re-called these early poems and the masks used in them? Despite Pound's own mental condition, the *Pisan Cantos* have not been considered the random notes of a confused mind for some time. It seems clear now that Pound had the time and the ability to craft them quite carefully, choosing the themes of the previous cantos which he wanted to elaborate here and the personae through which he could best accomplish that. Would Pound then—about to write his great post-war cantos—have recalled these very early examples of postwar poetry?

As mentioned earlier, the legend of Sweeney is just one of the stories that arose in the aftermath of the bloody Battle of Magh Rath. It is like the other tales of the Mad Celtic King, including the legend of King Goll, in that the madness itself is a direct result of Sweeney's experience at war. Even though the texts we have today, as I also mentioned earlier, tell us that Sweeney was sent into a frenzy under the curse of St. Ronan for attacking the church, several scholars—including J.G. O'Keeffe, who was the first to translate the legend into English—have argued that this curse is a later Christian revision of an essentially pagan tale. O'Keeffe suggests that the original story clearly attributed Sweeney's madness to "the horrors which he witnessed in the battle of Magh Rath" (xxxiv) and the text would seem to support this since the Irish monks failed to delete or alter crucial lines spoken by Sweeney such as: "Since the shock of battle / I'm a ghost of myself" (*SA* 29). In the Yeats poem, this is even clearer. The third stanza of the poem tells of the onset of Goll's madness in the midst of battle:

> But slowly, as I shouting slew
> And trampled in the bubbling mire,
> In my most secret spirit grew
> A whirling and a wandering fire:
> I stood: keen stars above me shone,
> Around me shone keen eyes of men:
> I laughed aloud and hurried on
> By rocky shore and rushy fen;
> I laughed because birds fluttered by,
> And starlight gleamed, and clouds flew high,
> And rushes waved and waters rolled. (*YP* 51–52)

Yeats later made clear that it was this version of the Goll legend that he had in mind, rather than those that suggested he had fallen in battle. Yeats explained that having reached the battle with extreme eagerness, [Goll's] excitement soon increased to frenzy, and after having performed astounding deeds of valour he fled in a state of derangement from the scene of the slaughter, and never stopped until he plunged into the wild seclusion of a deep glen far up in the country. (*YP* 492)

While Pound's own situation at Pisa was clearly different in that he did not participate directly in the fighting nor did he flee into the elements but was *thrown* into them, the opening lines of the *Pisan Cantos*—with their reference to "The enormous tragedy of the dream in the peasant's bent / shoulders" (74/425)—are intended to let the reader know that they too were written in the aftermath of a terrible and bloody battle. He speaks of the "po'eri di'aoli sent to the slaughter / Knecht gegen Knecht / to the sound of the bumm drum" (76/462–63), and in a line that almost echoes that of Sweeney himself who says, "woe to him who has slain by dint of his strength",[9] Pound proclaims, "woe to them that conquer with armies / and whose only right is their power" (76/463).

As is the case with the Mad Celtic Kings, the post-war torment for the lyric voice in the *Pisan Cantos* is as physical as it is emotional. Although Goll is forced to "wander wood and hill / through summer's heat and winter's cold," at least he has his "heavy locks" to shelter him (*YP* 52). Sweeney doesn't even have that. According to the versions of the tale handed on by the Irish monks, Sweeney's wife tried to restrain him as he ran from the house to confront the cleric and, though she got his royal cloak, she didn't get him, which prompted Ronan to declare:

> Bare to the world, here came Sweeney
> to harass and harrow me:
> therefore, it is God's decree
> bare to the world he'll always be.

> (*SA* 6)

However, Sweeney's physical torment is extremely touching. "Starved and mad," he describes himself as no more than

> a shape that flutters from the ivy
> to shiver under a winter sky,
> to go drenched in teems of rain
> and crouch under thunderstorms. (*SA* 22)

Pound's exposure to the elements at the camp at Pisa—first in the cage and then in the tent—would make for an interesting parallel if the images weren't so real. Like Sweeney, Pound can feel "the damp gnaw thru my bones" (74/429) and "fatigue deep as the grave" (83/533). The wind and the rain almost become characters in these cantos and even though Pound can appreciate the beauty of the green world, it is never without the knowledge that night follows day and cold follows warm and that Pound will be in it: in one line he can observe that

"Mist covers the breast of Tellus-Hellena and drifts up the Arno," but the next will state "came night and with night the tempest" (77/473). Like Sweeney, who has been unable to sleep since the Battle of Magh Rath, Pound finds it extremely difficult to rest, and it is not hard to imagine Sweeney's own lament coming from somewhere in the *Pisan Cantos* when he cries, "I freeze and burn. / I am the bare figure of pain" (*SA* 70).

For both Sweeney and Pound—as well as King Goll and Pound's mad troubadour—the physical suffering is accompanied by an equally severe mental and emotional suffering. Like Goll lifting his "mournful ulalu" and the troubadour protesting far too much that he is "gay," Sweeney points out in one of his saddest lyrics:

> My grief is raw and constant.
> To-night all my strength is gone.
> Who has more cause to lament
> than Mad Sweeney of Glen Bolcain?

> (*SA* 74)

Though the fragile state of Sweeney's mind has much to do with the effects of battle upon it, it is also clear that the strain is greatly increased by his isolation in the wilds. Though the plants and animals surrounding him can bring him as much comfort and company as they do Pound's mad troubadour, they also serve to remind him of just how alone he is and how much he has left behind. Sweeney laments this lost world:

> No house humming full,
> no men, loud with good will,
> nobody to call me king,
> no drink or banqueting.

> (*SA* 15)

He asks where is "The harper who harped me to rest, / where is his soothing music now?" (*SA* 48). Until his discovery of the green world and his celebration of it, the only relief for the Mad King—and for Goll in the Yeats poem—comes in the form of memory, of what he calls "dreaming back the good days" (43), memories of "curbing some great steed" (16), of camping with his troops the night before the Battle of Drumfree (20), of threatening to withdraw from the alliance before the Battle of Drum Lurgan and being begged and bribed to stay and fight, offered "in their hundreds / horses, bridles, swords, foreign / captives, girl attendants'' (59). But as Sweeney also notes, these memories are double-edged: while in these moments of reverie he can ''people the dark / with a thousand ghosts'' and find himself temporarily ''restored,'' they also quickly ''fade away'' and ''leave me to the night'' and alone (20–21), even becoming with time an enemy that sneaks up on him and taunts him, causing him to call these memories ''an unbroken horse / that rears and suddenly throws me down'' (48).

Pound's emotional and mental state at Pisa bears a striking resemblance to that of Sweeney. Like Sweeney, Pound feels isolated and alone, as though he has left an entire world behind him. He feels like ''a man on whom the sun has gone down'' (74/430), like ''a lone ant from a broken ant-hill'' (76/458), like one who has ''passed over Lethe'' (74/449). He feels completely separated from family and friends, and cries out to a bird in *Canto 76*:

> O white-chested martin, God damn it,
> as no one else will carry a message,
> say to La Cara: amo.
> (459)

As with Sweeney, the only temporary respite for Pound from this pain and isolation in the early *Pisan Cantos* is memory: memories of sitting beside the canal in Venice, thinking ''shd/I chuck the lot into the tide-water?'' (76/460), of ''Fordie that wrote of giants / and William who dreamed of nobility / and Jim the comedian singing'' (74/432–33), of ''the cake shops in the Nevsky, and Schöners / not to mention der Greif at Bolsano / la patronne getting older'' (74/433), of leaving America with eighty dollars in his pocket and England with ''a letter of Thomas Hardy's'' (80/500), of Edgar Williams in Verona (78/480) and Yeats in Paris (83/528), of ''the cat [that] walked the porch rail at Gardone'' (76/458) and ''the grass on the roof of St What's his name / near 'Cano e Gatto' . . . when they bless the wax for the Palio'' (83/529). As is the case with Sweeney, these memories are also double-edged in that they bring pain as well as pleasure: Pound begins to wonder ''who's dead, and who isn't / and will the world ever take up its course again?'' (76/453). There are also moments of extreme anguish, when cries of pain, alongside tears, make their way into the *Cantos*, including the shriek in *Canto 81*, which Pound's daughter has called ''an outburst more personal than any other in the *Cantos*'',[10] and which echoes the shriek uttered by the mad troubadour in Pound's early poem that precedes his recollection of the woman who sent him to the woods. In that poem, the memories of the woman are still so strong, despite his attempts to forget her, th he says he does not ''like to remember things any more'' (*CEP* 10). This double edge of memory becomes so acute at times that both Sweeney and Pound give in to thoughts of death, whether the ''instant'' at ''3 p.m.'' that Pound records in *Canto 82* (527) or Sweeney's admission that ''At times I am afraid'' (*SA* 17).

However, one of the great attractions of the Sweeney legend is that these moments of dark despair alternate with moments of celebration and exultation. And it is at these moments that the poetry really soars, that Sweeney discovers his lyric voice and his gift as a poet. This exultation is always linked with nature, and this is just as true in the story of King Goll as it is with Pound's mad troubadour or the lyric voice of the *Pisan Cantos*. While Pound's troubadour sings the praise of "the wind that flutters in the leaves" and claims that in the woods he has found "a great love / That is sweeter than the love of women" (*CEP* 9–10), Mad King Goll tells us that sometimes, even in the depths of winter when it is so cold that even "the cormorants shiver on their rocks," he merely waves his hands and sings (*YP* 52). Sweeney, once again, seems to be the model for such behavior. As Heaney has pointed out in an essay included in *Preoccupations*, the Mad King is a classic "foliate head," a "wood-lover and treehugger, a picker of herbs and drinker from wells".[11] Even though his expulsion to the wilds brings on the darkest of moods, it also gives him cause to rejoice as he discovers that he may have lost one kingdom, but he has found another: he says that at times the mere sound of a stag from the high cliff-tops, that echoes through the glen, can "ravish" him, describing it as an "Unearthly sweetness [that] shakes my breast" (*SA* 20). Even though he misses the kingly feasts, the company of friends and family, and the good wine that he used to drink, he is eventually able to say, "Watercress is my wealth, water is my wine, and hard bare trees and soft tree bowers are my friends" (46). It is in the discovery of this new world, this new kingdom, that Sweeney finds his poetic voice. Perhaps his most beautiful and lasting poetry comes in his famous praise of the trees and the other vegetation of the Irish countryside. Though I suppose it is impossible for non-Irish speakers to get a true sense of the quality of this verse—and I include myself here—Heaney has tried to capture its beauty in his version of the Sweeney legend:

> The bushy leafy oak tree
> is highest in the wood,
> the forking shoots of hazel
> hide sweet hazel-nuts.

> The alder is my darling,
> all thornless in the gap,
> some milk of human kindness
> coursing in its sap.

> The blackthorn is a jaggy creel
> stippled with dark sloes;

green watercress in thatch on wells
where the drinking blackbird goes.

Sweetest of the leafy stalks,
the vetches strew the pathway;
the oyster-grass is my delight,
and the wild strawberry. (36–37)

In his essay, Heaney argues that these lyrics are at the heart of early Irish nature poetry, a style of poetry that flourished long before the first monks began to write it down. Heaney notes that its "precision and suggestiveness" has often been compared to "the art of the Japanese *haiku*," even arguing that "Basho's frog plopping into its pool in seventeenth-century Japan makes no more durable or exact music than Belfast's blackbird clearing its throat over the lough almost a thousand years earlier" (181). Heaney describes this sort of poetry as "little jabs of delight in the elemental," and cites both O'Brien's reference to its "steel-pen exactness" and the Celtic scholar Kuno Meyer's claim that "To seek out and watch and love nature, in its tiniest phenomena as in its grandest, was given to no people so early and so fully as the Celt."[12]

Not only are these qualities the very same ones that Pound tried to restore to modern English poetry in the early days of Imagism—when he often cited Japanese *haiku* as a possible model—but they are also the sort of qualities that he returns to in the *Pisan Cantos*, particularly in those moments when he, like Sweeney, temporarily forgets his mental and physical torment and turns his attention outside himself. It is in these lyric moments that Pound—again like Sweeney, Goll, and his own mad troubadour—seems to let one world go for another. Although it would be difficult to argue that Pound *discovers* the green world for the first time in these cantos—as the Mad Kings and troubadours do—it can certainly be said that it is here that he *rediscovers* it, and although it would be even more ridiculous to argue that as a result of that Pound *discovers* his poetic nature here—as is the case with the Mad Celtic Kings—it can be said that it is in the *Pisan Cantos* that Pound *rediscovers* the sort of voice that he has rarely used since the early days of Imagism and that the rediscovery of this voice results in the creation of some of his finest lyrics. Like Sweeney and Goll, Pound begins to notice those things directly under his nose—as if for the very first time—whether it's the "smell of mint under the tent flaps" (74/428) or "two larks in contrappunto / at sunset" (74/431), whether "unexpected excellent sausage" (74/438) or the way "The shadow of the tent's peak" moves like a sundial (78/483), whether "the ideogram of the guard roosts" or "a white ox on the road toward Pisa" (74/428), whether the "Prowling night-puss" (80/498) or the wasp "building a very neat house / of four rooms, one shaped like a squat indian bottle'' (83/532). As Anthony Woodward has pointed out, if these minute observations have a ''religious emotion'' attached to them, it is a pagan rather than a Christian one (103) and, I might suggest, one that has much in common with the sort of ''religious emotion'' that one also feels in the descriptions of the external world in early Irish nature poetry, the poetry of Sweeney, and many of Yeats' and Pound's early poems.

This sense includes becoming aware of such simple everyday occurrences as the change from day to night, the sun rising and the sun setting. As the *Cantos* progress, the awareness expands to the change of seasons, from summer to autumn. One sort of awareness leads to another, and Pound begins to question, as Sweeney and Goll did before him, many of his previous assumptions concerning the conduct of life. Although he never says, as Sweeney eventually does, that he wouldn't trade his perch atop ''an ivy bush / high in some twisted tree'' for all the comforts of hearth and home (*SA* 41), Pound does undergo a change of character because of this experience. In *Canto 83*, for example, the simple act of observing how ''the ants seem to stagger / as the dawn sun has trapped their shadows'' and how the fog rests on the mountains (531), begins to suggest something far more significant to Pound:

> this breath wholly covers the mountains
>   it shines and divides
> it nourishes by its rectitude
> does no injury
> overstanding the earth it fills the nine fields
>   to heaven
>
> Boon companion to equity
>   it joins with the process
>   lacking it, there is inanition
>   (531)

This is the sort of aesthetic that Pound later sums up by stating that ''When the mind swings by a grass-blade/ an ant's forefoot shall save you'' (533).

However, as the *Canto* just cited suggests, it is not merely the discovery, or rediscovery, of the green world that is crucial to Pound here, but the discovery of his *place* in it. This, too, is one of the prime characteristics of the myth of the Mad Celtic King. As Heaney has noted, the celebration of the outside world in early Irish nature poetry is often linked with just such a discovery, a sense of one's place. He cites P.H. Henry's argument that this kind of poetry often goes hand-in-hand with another kind of poem which is its corollary and opposite, a kind we might characterize as penitential poetry. Both spring from a way of life at once simple and ascetic, the tensions of asceticism finding voice in the pentitential verse, and the cheerier nature lyrics springing from the solitary's direct experience of the changing seasons. (183) Although Heaney suggests that this sort of apposition may be due to a later Christian influence—"the sense of a spiritual principle and a religious calling that transcends the almost carnal lushness of nature itself" (183)—there are moments in the Sweeney legend when such a penitential mood takes hold of the Mad King without necessarily being linked to the Christian tradition. It is Sweeney's confrontation with nature that begins to bring the change in him. The same Mad King who was once so easy to anger can be heard saying:

> In November, wild ducks fly.
> From those dark days until May
> let us forage, nest and hide
> in ivy in the brown wood
>
> and hear behind birds' singing
> water sounds in Glen Bolcain,
> its fast streams, all hush and jabber,
> its islands on forking rivers,
>
> its hazel trees and holly bowers,
> its acorns and leaves and briars,
> its nuts, its sharp-tasting sloes,
> its sweet, cool-fleshed berries:
>
> and under trees, its hounds coursing,
> its loud stags bellowing,
> its waters' clear endless fall—
> what enmity is possible?

(*SA* 61–62)

Although Sweeney's penitence later takes the more Christian form of asking God's forgiveness for "Whatever evil I have done / in this world" (83), it is clear in the lines just cited that his change in character has more to do with his experience in the natural world than any sense of Christian duty.

In the later *Pisan Cantos*, there is a similar apposition between an almost pagan relish in the beauty of the world and a humbling awareness of one's place in it. This apposition is particularly evident in *Canto 81* where the close observation of the outside world leads directly into a sort of penitential verse:

> The ant's a centaur in his dragon world.

Pull down thy vanity, it is not man
Made courage, or made order, or made grace,
          Pull down thy vanity, I say pull down.
Learn of the green world what can be thy place
In scaled invention or true artistry,
Pull down thy vanity,
               Paquin pull down!
The green casque has outdone your elegance.
                    (521)

Pound makes it extremely clear in this section of the canto that this change of character is a direct result of his Sweeney-like exposure to the elements:

          Thou art a beaten dog beneath the hail,
          A swollen magpie in a fitful sun,
          Half black half white
          Nor knowst'ou wing from tail
          Pull down thy vanity
               How mean thy hates
          Fostered in falsity,
               Pull down thy vanity,
          Rathe to destroy, niggard in charity,
          Pull down thy vanity,
                    I say pull down.
                         (521)

Even though these lines are immediately followed by an extremely significant "but," it is clear that these cantos have completed the process that is so vital to the myth of the Mad Celtic King: thrown out-of-doors and exposed to all the elements of nature—wind and rain and cold—through extreme physical discomfort and mental strain, one world has been lost but another found and, consequently, a sense of one's place in it.

The question again comes back to whether or not this pattern is merely an accident of history or a direct borrowing from the Celtic myth, whether the lyric voice in these *Cantos* is to be identified exclusively as Pound's own or whether it is another of the many voices he uses. In either case, it seems somehow fitting that prior to his arrival at Stone Cottage, Dorothy Shakespear wrote to Pound that Georgie Hyde-Lees had "an amusing dream" about him. In the dream, Pound was perched very much in the manner of Sweeney atop a tree in Ashdown Forest. "You were hanging to the top of a very straight pine tree," she wrote, "and you had not climbed it—but got there 'by translation' as she says. You seemed very happy . . . and your hair was standing bolt upright, and was *very* long" (269). Had Yeats lived a decade longer, perhaps he would have appreciated the sad, prophetic truth of his wife's dream.

NOTES

1. James Longenbach, *Stone Cottage: Pound, Yeats, and Modernism* (Oxford: Oxford University Press, 1988), p. 10.

2. *Collected Early Poems of Ezra Pound*, ed. Michael John King (London: Faber, 1977), p. 8.

3. Yeats, "The Celtic Twilight" (1893) in *Early Poems and Stories* (London: Macmillan, 1925), p. 139.

4. Pound, *Collected Early Poems*, 8.

5. *Yeats's Poems*, ed. A. Norman Jeffares (London: Papermac, 1989), pp. 51–52.

6. Seamus Heaney, *Sweeney Astray* (London: Faber, 1984), p. 5.

7. Flann O'Brien, *At Swim-Two-Birds* (1939) (London: Penguin, 1967), p. 172.

8. Seamus Heaney, Introduction to his translation of *Sweeney Astray*.

9. *Buile Suibne: The Adventures of Suibhne Geilt*, translated by J.G. O'Keefe (London: Irish Texts Society, 1913), p. 145.

10. Mary de Rachewiltz, *Discretions* (London: Faber, 1971), p. 258.

11. Seamus Heaney, "The God in the Tree: Early Irish Nature Poetry," in *Preoccupations: Selected Prose 1968–1978* (London: Faber, 1984), p. 186.

12. Ibid., pp. 181–82.

8

WILLIAM PRATT
Pound's Hells, Real and Imaginary

When Ezra Pound was asked in a late interview where he was living now, he replied, "In Hell," and when asked "Which Hell?" he put his hand over his heart and answered "Here."[1] Pound was a major poet who wrote about major themes, with the poet's indispensable ear for what he called *melopoeia*, the music of words, but if his major themes included the worldly themes he listed in *Canto XI*:

> *de litteris et de armis, praestantibusque ingeniis,*
> Both of ancient times and our own; books, arms,
> And of men of unusual genius,
> Both of ancient times and our own, in short the usual subjects
> Of conversation between intelligent men,

they also included what all major Western poets starting with Homer have included, that is, visionary realms beyond the senses, most notably infernal regions, which are to be found in Homer and Vergil and Ovid as well as in Dante and Milton. Pound wrote of the "Thrones" or heavenly regions as well, but like the greatest poets of every age, he produced more infernal than ethereal images, meaning that evil seemed more real to him than good, or as he might have put it, poets write more often *diagnostically*, telling us what is wrong, than *therapeutically*, telling us what is right. By the end of *The Cantos*, Pound had been forced to recognize he was a "man seeking good/doing evil," and to confess that "my errors and wrecks lie about me," for "I have lost my center/ fighting the world." He had, however, in the course of his long career confronted evil over and over, at his highest moments objectifying it in memorable images of Hell that incorporate both the real suffering he knew as a man and the imaginary suffering he envisioned as a poet.

Pound admired Dante above all poets, and drew much of his inspiration from Dante's *Inferno*, the Hell of Hells in world poetry, beginning as early as his "Sestina: Altaforte" where, as his epigraph tells us, "Dante Alighieri put this man in hell for that he was a stirrer up of strife. Eccovi! Judge ye! Have I dug him up again?" It is a question most readers would answer in the affirmative, for Pound did achieve his aim of bringing the much-admired Provencal troubadour Bertrand de Born to life again out of Dante's Hell. But his imaginary

journey to Hell also received early inspiration from the Classical Roman poet
Propertius. In two different poems Pound creatively translated Propertius' ele-
giac Latin into memorable English. The first of these Hell images occurs in
Pound's earliest *Personae* volume, dating from 1910:

Prayer for His Lady's Life
From Propertius, Elegiae, lib. II, 26

Here let thy clemency, Persephone, hold firm,
Do thou, Pluto, bring here no greater harshness.
So many thousand beauties are gone down to Avernus,
Ye might let one remain above with us.

With you is Iope, with you the white-gleaming Tyro,
With you is Europa and the shameless Pasiphae,
And all the fair from Troy and all from Achaia,
From the sundered realms, of Thebes and of aged Priamus;
And all the maidens of Rome, as many as they were,
They died and the greed of your flame consumes them.

Here let thy clemency, Persephone, hold firm
Do thou, Pluto, bring here no greater harshness.
So many thousand fair are gone down to Avernus,
Ye might let one remain above with us.

This translation distinguishes itself from many other early Pound translations
by taking the subject of Hell seriously and envisioning it as a final resting place
of beautiful women. But when Pound put together a set of translations from the
Latin poet in 1917, in twelve sections that make up his first long poem, *Homage
to Sextus Propertius*, he revised his earlier version considerably and made a
better poem of it, fitting it into the longer work as Section IX, Part 2:

Persephone and Dis, Dis, have mercy upon her,
There are enough women in hell,
                              quite enough beautiful women,
Iope, and Tyro, and Pasiphae, and the formal girls of Achaia,
And out of Troad, and from the Campania,
Death has his tooth in the lot,
                              Avernus lusts for the lot of them,
Beauty is not eternal, no man has perennial fortune,
Slow foot, or swift foot, death delays but for a season.

In this condensed translation of Propertius's Elegy, Hell becomes a more active force of death, a masculine Avernus "lusting" for mortal women whom he carries down to the lower depths, just as Pluto or Dis had carried Persephone to Hell in the Greekmyth, and Pound reinforces the theme of mortality by picturing a Hell filled with "quite enough beautiful women," yet still seeking more, seeking even Propertius' mistress Cynthia. So Pound improved upon his earlier translation of Propertius and at the same time increased the potency of his vision of Hell, showing that he had become a more mature poet in the decade between them.

However, the most profound and moving vision of Hell to be found in the *Homage to Sextus Propertius*, and indeed in all of Pound's poetry prior to the *Cantos*, is Section VI, worth quoting in full because it describes both the dead and the living:

> When, when, and whenever death closes our eyelids,
> Moving naked over Acheron
> Upon the one raft, victor and conquered together,
> Marius and Jugurtha together,
>   one tangle of shadows.
> Caesar plots against India,
> Tigris and Euphrates shall, from now on, flow at his bidding,
> Tibet shall be full of Roman policemen,
> The Parthians shall get used to our statuary
>   and acquire a Roman religion;
> One raft on the veiled flood of Acheron,
>   Marius and Jugurtha together.
> Nor at my funeral either will there be any long trail,
>   bearing ancestral lares and images;
> No trumpets filled with my emptiness,
> Nor shall it be on an Attalic bed;
>
>   The perfumed cloths shall be absent.
> A small plebeian procession
>   Enough, enough and in plenty
> There will be three books at my obsequies
> Which I take, my not unworthy gift, to Persephone.
>
> You will follow the bare scarified breast
> Nor will you be weary of calling my name, nor too weary
>   To place the last kiss on my lips
> When the Syrian onyx is broken

"He who is now vacant dust
Was once the slave of one passion;"
Give that much inscription
"Death why tardily come?"

You, sometimes, will lament a lost friend,
For it is a custom:
This care for past men,

Since Adonis was gored in Idalia, and the Cytherean
Ran crying with out-spread hair,
In vain, you call back the shade,
In vain, Cynthia. Vain call to unanswering shadow,
Small talk comes from small bones.

Pound never worded his description of Hell more vividly anywhere in his poetry than in this section of a poem which is as much an original as a translation: it is Pound plus Propertius, the twentieth century A.D. American poet echoing the first century B.C. Roman poet, but adding his own phrases and twists of irony to the elegant irony of the Latin poet. Rather than picturing the many mythical beauties in Hell, Pound pictures the historical Roman general Marius and his vanquished African opponent Jugurtha, figures out of Roman history in the century before Propertius, but seen as joined in death on the same "raft," that is, on Charon's boat crossing the Acheron to Hell with dead souls aboard it, as it was portrayed by Vergil in Book 6 of his *Aeneid* and again by Dante in the Third Canto of his *Inferno*, but neither Vergil nor Dante pictured the souls of Marius and Jugurtha on Charon's boat. Pound speaks for Propertius, a dead soul already, who imagines his mistress Cynthia attending his funeral and trying to call him back from the dead, but in vain, since he will be only "unanswering shadow" then and her plea will be unheard, for—in the moving pathos of the poem—"small talk comes from small bones." Pound has converted Propertius' Classical image of Hell from a place under the earth after death to a state of mind during life, for all those who can imagine a Hell before death.

What Pound accomplished in *Propertius* was to bring Hell forward from ancient belief to contemporary relevance, making it personal as well as universal, expressing regret for the mortality of all human beings and at the same time expressing the anticipation of death as a common fate for all who have ever lived, the victorious hero as well as his defeated enemy, the poet as well as his beloved, and thus offering some consolation in a death which no one can escape, yet grief nevertheless for the loss of heroes as well as lovers, generals as well as poets. Though Pound subscribed to neither pagan nor Christian religious creed in his depiction of Hell, he was clearly seized with a vision of Hell from his earliest years and it never left him, becoming more and more fully realized in his "forty-year epic" of *The Cantos* which really took him fifty years to complete, carrying him all the way from the first *Cantos* and *Homage to Sextus Propertius* in 1917 to the final *Drafts and Fragments of Cantos* in 1968.

Pound spoke of two main themes in his *Cantos*: the descent of a living man into Hell, and the moment of Metamorphosis or vision; in other words, he divided his version of Dante's *Divine Comedy* into two realms, Hell and Heaven, with no real Purgatory—unless his Purgatory was a state alternating between Heaven and Hell. Pound had written as early as 1910, in his chapter on Dante in *The Spirit of Romance*, that "Dante conceived the real Hell, Purgatory, and Paradise as states, not places," [2] and so when he modelled his *Cantos* on Dante's epic poem, he meant his poem to be consistent with Dante as he understood him. Dante, in his view, showed that "Hell is the state of man dominated by his passions, who has lost 'the good of the intelligence.' " [3] In Pound's modern epic, Hell is most often portrayed as a place of darkness governed by men who are driven by "money-lust" or *usura*, (in 1934, responding to Laurence Binyon's new translation of the *Inferno*, Pound asserted that "the whole hell reeks with money") while Heaven is a place of light governed by a ruler like Confucius or Thomas Jefferson who encourages the arts and philosophy to flourish: to simplify Pound's very complex poem, Hell is damned by money, the material root of all evil; Heaven is glorified by art, the spiritual sublimation of all good.

Pound's *Cantos* begin, not with Dante but with Homer, at the very beginning of Western literature, with the journey to Hell of Ulysses in Book 11 of *The Odyssey*. *Canto I* consists mostly of a translation of Homer's Greek, filtered through the medium of an obscure medieval Latin translator named Andreas Divus, and infused with the rhythm of Anglo-Saxon meter, the alliterative four-beat line of *Beowulf* and "The Seafarer" and "The Wanderer":

> And then went down to the ship,
> Set keel to breakers, forth on the godly sea, and
> We set up mast and sail on that swart ship,
> Bore sheep aboard her, and our bodies also
> Heavy with weeping, and winds from sternward
> Bore us out onward with bellying canvas,
> Circe's this craft, the trim-coifed goddess.

Pound follows Homer's story only so far as Ulysses goes in his journey to receive the prophecy of Teiresias that will guide him in his return to his native island of Ithaca—less than half of Book 11 of *The Odyssey*—but it serves Pound's purpose of descending into Hell with Ulysses so that he, the American poet of the twentieth century, can fashion an epic poem that will become his homeland and the fulfillment of his vision. He breaks off the first Canto by bringing in Aphrodite, the Greek goddess of love, and the Golden Bough of Argicida, or Hermes, that symbol of immortality which Aeneas in Book 6 of Vergil's epic, *The Aeneid*, found with the guidance of the Sibyl of Cumae and the help of his mother, the goddess Venus, to lead him safely through Hades. Thus Pound's poem begins with a gesture of appreciation both to Homer and to Vergil, epic poets of Greece and Rome whose heroes Ulysses and Aeneas had long ago made their journeys to Hell.

Pound does not bring Dante directly into his poem until *Cantos XIV* through *XVI*, his Hell Cantos, and *Canto XLV*, his Usury Canto, but when he envisions his own imaginary Inferno, he does not stint: it is thoroughly disgusting, flowing with excrement and overwhelmed with greed. In fact, *Cantos XIV* and *XV* suffer in comparison with Dante because they are dominated by unrelieved obscenity, "without dignity, without tragedy," ditches full of besmutted bishops and lady golfers wallowing in slime, but as Eliot observed in *After Strange Gods*: "Mr. Pound's Hell, for all its horrors, is a perfectly comfortable one for the modern mind to contemplate, and disturbing to no one's complacency: it is a Hell for the *other people*, the people we read about in newspapers, not for oneself and one's friends."[4] Eliot's remark may have prompted Pound himself to say in his essay on Cavalcanti shortly afterward (1934):

> This invention of hells for one's enemies, and mess, confusion
> in sculpture is always symptomatic of supineness, bad hygiene,
> bad physique (possibly envy); even the diseases of mind, they
> do not try to cure as such but devise hells to punish, not to
> heal, the individual sufferer.

Apparently Pound realized that he might have gone too far in punishing his enemies in *Cantos XIV* and *XV*, moving dangerously close to the "hell-obsession" he denounced in other poets, but *Canto XVI* is written in another dimension, appearing at first to place him in Purgatory, "before hell mouth; dry plain and two mountains," but quickly descending again into "The limbo of chopped ice and saw-dust" and then into war as Hell— specifically, World War I, to which many of Pound's friends went, some of them to be killed. He mentions Richard Aldington, his fellow Imagist poet, and Henri Gaudier-Brzeska, the French sculptor killed in the war, and T.E. Hulme, the founder of the original School of Images, who took library books with him to the trenches—Pound notes humorously that the library complained—but who also was killed, and then Wyndham Lewis, the editor of the shortlived Vorticist magazine *Blast*: all these fellow-artists were drawn into the folly of war, and Pound's anger is directed at those who led their nations into war and profited from it while many talented men were lost. *Canto XVI* contains deeper human interest than the two preceding Hell Cantos, and is an eloquent protest against war as man's creation of a Hell on earth.

What most creates Hell on earth for Pound is usury, and in one of his best-known *Cantos, XLV*, he denounces Dante's previously cursed *Usura*, or excessive profit-making, as materialism or money-worship, "with usura, sin against nature,/is thy bread ever more of stale rags,/is thy bread dry as paper," and he gives a ringing litany of all the artists whose works were not made for monetary gain but for the love of art and in celebration of the immortal spirit in man. They are almost all Renaissance Italian painters and architects, except for the anonymous French architects of the Romanesque basilicas of St. Trophime in Arles and St. Hilaire in Poitiers, and the Flemish painter Hans Memling. Pound's poem is a splendid example of the rhetorical technique of *polysyndeton*, or successive and repeated coordination, and it reads like the impassioned denunciation of sin by a Hebrew prophet, but it is largely the exaltation of artists who succeeded despite Usury in creating great works of art—quite different in character from the Usura Canto of Dante, who pictures his sinners suffering punishments in Hell for their unnatural greed.

In the following *Canto XLVI*, Pound makes light of "you who think you will/get through hell in a hurry," having already used *Cantos I, XIV-XVI,* and *XLV* to comprise his image of Hell, borrowing from Homer, Vergil, and Dante to portray a composite state of man governed by passion more than reason, mixing mythical as well as historical characters from the past with his own contemporaries in the present, denouncing as sins chiefly the folly and destruction of war and the corruption of greed, but showing that some are able to pass through Hell unscathed, like Ulysses and Aeneas in the past and Aldington and Lewis in the present, Pound himself as artist experiencing but surviving the Hell he creates.

He was by no means getting through hell in a hurry, for he began *Canto XLVII* with a sounding reprise of Ulysses' journey to hell in the first *Canto*:

> Who even dead, yet hath his mind entire!
> This sound came in the dark
> First must thou go the road
>   to hell
> And to the bower of Ceres' daughter Proserpine,
> Through overhanging dark, to see Tiresias,
> Eyeless that was a shade, that is in hell
> So full of knowing that the beefy men know less than he,
> Ere thou come to thy road's end.

He then added substantially to the earlier Hell Cantos, written mainly in English, with two later Hell Cantos written in Italian during the Second World War. *Cantos LXXII* and *LXXIII* are his nearest equivalents to Dante's *Inferno*, the model for his entire sequence, though Pound's Italian is much more colloquial and less lyrical than Dante's. The Italian Cantos are most like his own earlier *Canto XVI*, in that war is their major subject, but they are unlike the earlier Hell Cantos in that they focus on particular figures, as Dante did, first Pound's own contemporary and friend, Tomaso Marinetti, the founder of Futurism, in *Canto LXXII*, and then Dante's contemporary and friend, Guido Cavalcanti, in *Canto LXXIII*.

    Canto LXXII brings the recently dead Marinetti, who like Pound had been a supporter of Mussolini, into ghostly touch with Pound: he audaciously asks for Pound's body to continue his fight. Pound refuses on the ground that his body is old and besides he still needs it, but he salutes Marinetti in parting with the assertion *ch'io faccia il canto della guerra eterna/Fra luce e fango—* "that I have made the song of the eternal war between light and mud"—and wishes him a hearty farewell, "Addio, Marinetti!" The remaining lines bring in other figures less vividly: Sigismondo da Malatesta and Galla Placidia from earlier *Cantos*, and Ezzelina da Romano from Dante's *Inferno*, all of whom confirm that the war is still going on and that he must continue to sing about it.

    Canto LXXIII allows Pound to revive Guido Cavalcanti, Dante's friend and fellow-poet, much admired and translated by Pound early in his career. Cavalcanti appears as a ghost on horseback ("Cavalcanti" means "horseman" in Italian), who tells Pound that he has ridden past Rimini, where Sigismondo's Tempio is threatened by the advancing Allied armies, and has seen a young Italian woman heroically avenge her rape by a troop of Canadian soldiers, dying with them in a minefield explosion into which she leads them: *All'inferno 'l nemico,/furon venti morti,/Morta la ragazza*: "twenty dead enemy soldiers sent to Hell, and the girl dead, too," "*ma che ragazza!*"—"but what a girl!" he exclaims admiringly—and then Cavalcanti recalls where he has come from, "*Io tornato son'/dal terzo cielo*," "I've returned from the Third Heaven" of Venus, still marveling at the bravery of the Italian girl he has seen on the battlefield of the Second World War.

    The Italian Cantos carry forward Pound's imagery of Hell into the later Cantos, but the culmination is to be found in the *Pisan Cantos*, where the imprisonment of Pound himself in the army detention camp at Pisa, condemned by American soldiers to live in the "gorilla cage" or barred enclosure open to the weather, as a traitor to his own country for his broadcasts over Rome Radio in the Second World War, "a lone ant from a broken anthill," gives the most compelling sense of the state of man "dominated by his passions, who has lost 'the good of the intelligence' " as he saw the souls in Dante's *Inferno*.

> If the hoar frost grip thy tent
> Thou wilt give thanks when night is spent

Pound's moving account of his humiliation and actual physical suffering in the prison cage at Pisa places him in the Ninth Circle of the *Inferno*, where the traitor Count Ugolino (who betrayed Pisa) became a cannibal, through forced starvation in the tower where he was imprisoned—"shall we look for a deeper or is this the bottom?/ Ugolino, the tower there on the tree line"—and still lower down, Judas and Brutus and Cassius writhe in the mouth of Satan. Pound does not explicitly compare himself, as a traitor to his country, to these arch-traitors in Dante's poem, but the analogy cannot escape those who read Pound with Dante in mind. Finally, however, Pound is able by the power of his imagination to transcend his real earthly Hell, affirming unforgettably in *Canto LXXXI*:

> First came the seen, then thus the palpable
> Elysium, though it were in the halls of hell,
> What thou lovest well is thy true heritage.

Pound, in other words, was able through his imagination to find a place of blessedness in a place of torment, just as Aeneas in Vergil's epic found Elysium in Hades, a Heaven in the midst of Hell. Furthermore, Pound can attest in lines of exquisite lyricism that poetry, "what thou lovest well," is possible even in the worst conditions imaginable, as he proved by the superb poetry he wrote at Pisa and later in the asylum of St. Elizabeths in Washington, among them the lines of *Canto 90* of *Section: Rock-Drill*, where "out of Erebus, the deep-lying/ from the wind under the earth, m'elevasti," ["I lift myself up"]—further proof of Pound's astonishing ability to transcend his personal, real Hell. As H.D., anointed by Pound as the original Imagist, would later attest in her tribute, *End to Torment: A Memoir of Ezra Pound*, "There is a reserve of dynamic or dae-monic power from which we may all draw. He lay on the floor of the iron cage and wrote *The Pisan Cantos*."[5] Pound's triumph over adversity comes through his poetic gift, in spite of the shame and the madness:

> To have gathered from the air a live tradition,
> Or from a fine old eye the unconquered flame,
> This is not vanity.

Like earlier epic poets who wrote of Hell, like Homer and Vergil and Dante, Pound made poetry out of his own physical and mental torment, and he presented an original and forceful modern image of Hell, above all in the *Pisan Cantos*, where the power of his imagination enabled him to see "Elysium, though it were in the halls of hell."

Of course, it can be said that Pound never really transcended Hell, that is, Evil and Death and Madness. To those who visited him during his long stay at St. Elizabeths, he liked to refer to himself as "Grampa in the bughouse," and he admitted in the last *Drafts and Fragments of Cantos* that he became in his old age a "blown husk that is finished," who like Ulysses had "lost all companions," just as Teiresias in Hades predicted in the first Canto. In fact Pound became less like Homer's Ulysses, who emerged alive from Hell and returned alone to his home in Ithaca, and more like Dante's Ulysses, who in *Canto XXVI* of the *Inferno* sails from Ithaca into unknown seas beyond the Gates of Hercules and is shipwrecked and drowned at the foot of Mt. Purgatory, exceeding the limits set for mortals and deserving to be placed himself in one of the lowest regions of Hell rather than among the fallen heroes in Purgatory or among the saints in Paradise. As Pound told Donald Hall in an interview in 1960,

> It is difficult to write a paradiso when all the superficial indications are that you ought to write an apocalypse. It is obviously much easier to find inhabitants for an inferno or even a purgatorio.[6]

We can say that Pound finished his poem more or less hopelessly, without Dante's redeeming vision of Heaven as the Heart of Light, but to say so does not leave him in the lowest region of Hell, to which he seems to consign himself in *The Pisan Cantos*. No reader can forget that Pound had the power to imagine Heaven even in Hell, and if he admitted "Many errors,/a little rightness,/to excuse his hell [that is, Dante's]/and my paradiso," he ended his epic with a touching prayer of penitence:

> Let the Gods forgive what I
> have made

If Pound's Hell was real as well as imaginary, lasting all the way through *The Cantos*, he could still speak wistfully at the end

> about that terzo
> third heaven,
> that Venere
> again is all "paradiso"
> a nice quiet paradise
> over the shambles

So if, at the end of his life, Pound bore witness that he was living in Hell, and the Hell was inside his heart, in death, at least, he held the hope that he might join the ghost of Guido Cavalcanti, the poet whom Pound envisioned in *Canto LXXIII* as saying, *Io tornato son'/dal terzo cielo*: "I've come back from the Third Heaven."

NOTES

1. Donald Hall, *Remembering Poets: Reminiscences and Opinions*, (New York: Harper Colophon Books, 1978), p. 191.

2. Ezra Pound, *The Spirit of Romance* (1910, New York: New Directions, n.d.), p. 128.

3. Ibid, p. 129.

4. T.S. Eliot, *After Strange Gods: A Primer of Modern Heresy* (London: Faber, 1934), p. 43.

5. H.D., *End to Torment: A Memoir of Ezra Pound* (New York: New Directions, 1979), p. 44.

6. Donald Hall, *Remembering Poets*, op. cit, p. 241.

9

PETER NICHOLLS

Against Nature: Time and Artifice in Pound's Early Work

In the passage from his invention of imagism to the opening stages of *The Cantos*, Pound seems to have reformulated his understanding of *time*, shifting from a poetics of loss and nostalgia for origins, to one in which a sort of bracketing of origins made possible a newly active relation of poet to history. Indeed, a reading of the early work shows Pound becoming increasingly fascinated by the ways in which the writing of history is also a rewriting, a reinscription of the past. Such writing is a product of both memory and fantasy, and is shaped by the interaction of past and present. As Freud said in his study of the Wolf Man (a study almost contemporary with imagism), "these scenes from infancy are not reproduced during the treatment as recollection, they are the products of construction."[1] That idea of "construction" may have some bearing on Pound's developing sense of the past and its texts; at least I want to suggest that his concept of time is *formally* quite distinct from those continuous, natural temporal rhythms which occupy such a prominent *thematic* place in *The Cantos*.

We can find intimations of this development in Pound's early verse, where anachronism plays an important part. At this point, though, it operates primarily at the level of theme, associating the poet's own sense of a literal (and, of course, chosen) "exile" from the land of his birth with a more generalized, Paterian mood of "homesickness" for an earlier age. Poems like "In Durance" dramatize this feeling of alienation by evoking in Yeatsian style those "far halls of memory"[2] in which the echoes of a more habitable past seem still to resonate. To review Pound's early volumes with this theme in mind is to be struck by the way in which images of transcendental estrangement are coupled with those of narcissism. In "Plotinus", for example:

> But I was lonely as a lonely child.
> I cried amid the void and heard no cry,
> And then for utter loneliness, made I
> New thoughts as crescent images of *me*.
> And with them was my essence reconciled
> While fear went forth from mine eternity.

One reason for Pound's frequent recourse to stylistic pastiche in the early poems is perhaps that it offered a way of moving beyond this self-reflecting poetics, by making the writer seem merely the passive vehicle and conduit for images deriving from "the great dead days."[3] Such poems couple the imagery of a sensuous Platonism with the formal device of reminiscence, but they derive their consolatory power from a capacity to efface the poetic self which is otherwise felt to be trapped in the closed moment of modernity: "How our modernity,/ Nerve-wracked and broken, turns/Against time's way and all the way of things,/ Crying with weak and egoistic cries!"[4] This view of the self is expressed almost programmatically in the early poem "Histrion" where Pound conjures with the idea that "the souls of all men great/At times pass through us,/And we are melted into them, and are not/Save reflexions of their souls."[5] Here the Paterian aesthetic of the arrested moment allows the past to return, but it does so at the expense of the poetic sensibility which is invaded or possessed by it. The present tense of the poem is eclipsed by the fantasy of a return to origins: "So cease we from all being for the time,/And these, the Masters of the Soul, live on."

Now it is easy to see how this essentially passive model of the poetic self, as nostalgic and trapped in narcissistic forms of desire, came to be identified by Pound with an equally passive epistemology which he labelled "impressionism." He objects to impressionism partly because of its links to empiricist psychologies for which the impression is merely a trace deposited in the mind by a previous experience, leaving art to re-present that trace so precisely that the intervening passage of time will be obliterated. The campaign for Imagism was, in one respect, an attempt to achieve a more concentrated sense of a collision of time-schemes, though in its first format the image was still tied to a late romantic convention of writing about special moments. Within early modernism, Pater's "moment" had become the "impression" of Conrad and Ford Madox Ford. What is particularly important about the distinction between "image" and "impression" is that the "impression" is typically unmixed. Its intensity results from its capacity to make one moment govern an emotional state. As Ford put it in his key essay "On Impressionism," "to import into the record of observations of one moment the observations of a moment altogether different is not Impressionism. For Impressionism is a thing altogether momentary."[6]

It was, however, precisely this interaction of different moments which interested Pound, and his use of juxtaposition suggested a way of making a formal hiatus or pause—a gap between two parts of the poem—a space in which the reader might construe relationship. This conception of the image also contained in germ Pound's evolving notion of translation as a kind of model for the writing process itself—translation, that is, as a form of reinscription which allows past and present languages to exist in tension with each other. Such "Making It New" thus offered release from that world of the early poems in which desire was inextricably colored by nostalgia and loss, and where the poem was always the unhappy copy of some lost original. Pound's new habit of drawing parallels between poetry and the visual arts was closely bound up with this development, providing him with literal figures for the juxtapositional play of anachrony (as "planes in relation") *and* for a desire which is properly externalized in a world of objects. The spatial metaphor thus offered Pound a way of thinking the stylised temporal relation which would govern writing-as-translation. Now what is of particular interest about this pivotal moment in Pound's career is that it coincided with his work on Japanese Noh. It was in those plays, I think, that Pound suddenly discovered a spatial embodiment of this anachronous sense of time. We know that between 1914 and 1916 he frequently thought of Noh as a possible model for "a long imagiste or vorticist poem,"[7] partly because it exemplified what he called "Unity of Image" (*Noh*, 27):

> In the best "Noh" the whole play may consist of one image.
> I mean it is gathered about one image. Its unity consists in
> one image, enforced by movement and music. I see nothing
> against a long vorticist poem.[8]

In contrast, though, to Fenollosa's description of the Noh play's use of a centralized metaphor to produce a unified, organic structure, Pound's account is already linked to his new sense of the "moving" as opposed to the "fixed" image. What that entailed would soon be clear from the first drafts of *The Cantos*, where the image as static "equation" for a particular mood would be recast as a device of reference and allusion which would hold in tension the various materials of the poem. Such a process is metonymic rather than metaphoric, and is clearly in line with Pound's recognition that "The art of allusion, or this love of allusion in art, is at the root of the Noh." (*Noh*, 4) The emotion is, as Yeats put it, "self-conscious and reminiscent, always associating itself with pictures and poems" (p.160), and the "intensification" of the Noh image prized by Pound would thus produce results which were quite different from the centralizing of a particular mood in the imagist mode.

What then of the large-scale structure of Noh? According to Pound, "The Noh service presents, or symbolizes, a complete diagram of life and recurrence" (pp.11–12). The "diagram" refers to the traditional presentation of five plays in sequence, though this does not entail any rigid closure. In contrast to linear Western concepts of "form," the Noh cycle turns back on itself, always seeming to begin again (one critic, Kunio Komparu, observes that the last play in the sequence is not "a final conclusion, but a temporary cutoff that might even be considered the beginning of an endless succession"[9]). Yet while this lack of closure is associated with the Buddhist theory of salvation,[10] binding together natural and supernatural worlds in a rhythm of "recurrence," Noh theater also employs *discordant* structures which are actually quite removed from the fluid and predictable rhythms of a phantasmatic "nature". Such structures are intimately related to the extreme stylization of Noh which Pound and Yeats so much admired, producing temporal rhythms which, we might say, rewrite nature as artifice. Indeed, "recurrence" in this context has a second meaning, since many of the plays which Pound and Yeats presented embody the trope of a return, but a momentary return from death to life. This, then, is the time of the *super*natural which, far from being cyclical and predictable, entails, as Pound puts it, "the suspense of waiting for a supernatural manifestation" (p.26), a manifestation, he goes on to observe, of the interpenetration of past and present. What exactly does this "interpenetration" entail? The question goes to the heart of Noh, one of whose two main forms, *mugen-noh*, or "the Noh of spirits," (p.54) as Pound calls it, requires what Komparu terms "the reflection-in-vision method (*mugen-kaiso-ho*), in which the flow of time within the play is reversed and takes place in a memory or dream."[11] This convention of reversed time produces a ritual (not to say "diagrammatic") narrative structure. The leading figure of the play (the *shite*) appears as an old man or woman who is engaged in conversation by the secondary figure or *waki*, usually a priest. They discourse about a famous legend of the place, whereupon the *shite* reveals that he or she is in fact the character in the tale. The *shite* then disappears, only to return to the stage in the form of the legendary figure. The second part of the play—often preceded by a brief farce or Kyogen performance—presents the *waki*'s dream in which the *shite* dances. As Nobuko Tsukui observes, "The highlight of the *mugen-noh* is the tale and dance of the Shite in both forms . . . Its subject matter varies, but its form does not—the *mugen-noh* takes the form of a reminiscence of the Shite."[12]

Tsukui's emphasis on reminiscence is very much to the point here, since a peculiarity of this type of Noh is that its main action takes place at once in the present of the play's performance *and* in the past of stylized recollection (the dream of the *waki*). The visionary second part of the play thus links the manifestation of the god or spirit with the irruption of the past in the present, making the point of greatest intensity that in which time flows back on itself and two moments are, as it were, superimposed or grafted together. The unity of the play is discordant in the sense that the action entails two different chronologies, even though the characters are the same. As Komparu puts it, "dramatic time is split and revolves around two axes."[13] This "splitting" involves more than a simple juxtaposition of past and present, for the reversal of chronology produces a sort of compound tense in which the past may seem open to change or revision. *Mugen-noh*, as Komparu observes, "always follows a stream of consciousness . . . in which the remembered past and the actual present are fused into a whole *that advances both at the same time*."[14] The past, then, is not simply recalled (as a representation), but may be modified and transformed through its (re-)enactment. Komparu notes that "We might say that a drama of reminiscence acts out the past after the present, and that time must overcome the natural flow and run in reverse."[15] The unnatural "split" time of Noh thus offered Pound a model of a structure which folds back on itself, becoming in that movement a sort of allegory of its own process.[16]

In line with Komparu's argument that past and present are fused together and advanced "*both at the same time*," plays such as *Kinuta* and *Kagekiyo* use the reversal of time as a means of redemption. In *Kinuta*, for example, a wife who dies of grief because of her errant husband is called back from death by the force of his grief and repentance. Here time flows backwards to release the woman from the repetition symbolically associated with the fulling board which she beats throughout the years of her husband's absence; the play ends in spiritual resolution: "Her constant beating of silk has opened the flower, even so lightly she has entered the seed-pod of Butsu" (*Noh*, p.97). Such moments of doctrinal wisdom appealed to Pound less, however, than those examples of Noh in which the collision of past and present produced an unexpected transformation of both through the force of desire rather than through Buddhist belief.

Partly for this reason, Zeami's *Nishikigi* assumed a special importance for Pound.[17] Here a priest meets a woman carrying "a cloth woven of feathers" and a man with a "staff or a wooden sceptre/Beautifully ornate" (*Noh*, p.77). The priest learns that this man's staff or charm-stick is a token which may be left outside a woman's house as a sign of love for her. If, as is the case in *Nishikigi*, the woman refuses her suitor she ignores the stick. The priest is then taken to the burial mound of the man who had left charm-sticks outside the woman's house for three years and had still failed to win her love. As the second scene of the play opens, the ghosts of the couple appear in the priest's dream and the man dances to celebrate the happiness he and the woman have found together in death.

In many respects, *Nishikigi* is of the plays translated by Pound the clearest example of Komparu's account of Noh time-schemes. Here the conjunction of past and present moves both into a new phase; the past, we might say, is transformed by being remembered. In reality, as the *shite* recalls in the first part of the play, "We had no meeting together," but in the priest's dream which provides the frame for the second part the past can be, as it were, rewritten. As the ghost of the woman says:

> Aïe, honoured priest!
> You do not dip twice in the river
> beneath the same tree's shadow
> Without bonds in some other life.
> Hear soothsay,
> Now is there meeting between us,
> Between us who were until now
> In life and in after-life kept apart.

> (*Noh*, pp.81–82)

As in *Kinuta*, the reversal of time through the exercise of
memory in the first part of the play produces not repetition but
something new:

> To dream under dream we return.
> Three years . . . And the meeting comes now!
> This night has happened over and over,
> And only now comes the tryst.

As the play comes to a close it is as if we are caught between two times, a past
of repetition and a present which celebrates its reworking. The austere stylization
of Noh is thus governed by a profound displacement of emotion, not simply as
a translation of intensity into disciplined gesture, but by its habitual way of
expressing feeling through reminiscence. Emotion is felt retroactively, suggesting
that the past can be completed only in the present, and—more doctrinally—that
life can be known only from the vantage-point of death (Yeats was thus led to
remark that "It is even possible that being is only possessed completely by the
dead" [*Noh*, p.155][18]).

Such plays turn back to the past in order to prevent us from compulsively
repeating it, providing in that trope of a ghostly return a means by which to
refigure that which obsesses us. In just this way, translation functions to supplement its original, at once adding to and completing the text on which it works.[19]
Like Noh spirits, these texts "come back" belatedly, *nachträglich*, in Freud's
sense of the deferred action by which a traumatic experience takes on its full
meaning only at a later stage ("the articulation of two *moments* with a time of
delay," as one commentator neatly puts it[20]). Viewed from this perspective,
Pound's injunction to "Make It New" signals not simply an idea of cultural
renovation but a far more complex process by which two different times are
grafted together, each somehow "supplementing" the other. *The Cantos* were
to become a "palimpsest" in which, ideally, one text might overlay another
without effacing it.[21]

II

For all Pound's attraction, then, to myths of natural process and to
rhythms of cyclical recurrence, the temporal structures which come to govern
his own work are deliberately artificial, creating forms of discontinuity which he
actually thinks of in strongly *spatial* terms. As we have seen, such discontinuities
undermine a metaphysics of origin, freeing the poet from contemplative immer-
sion in some idealized past and allowing him instead to construe its texts as
objects to be worked upon and reworked in the present. An occult waiting upon

spirits is now replaced by the figure of the poet-as-sculptor, for like the sculptor the poet exercises a certain force of stylistic mastery "against nature." The spatial metaphor becomes increasingly important as Pound begins work on *The Cantos*, for more than ever he is aware of the need not to reproduce the past— "the classics in paraphrase", an aesthetics of essence and resemblance—but to activate something "new," which will result from a dynamic interaction of past and present.

Now we are used to thinking about this important phase of Pound's work as an especially directed and purposeful one in which he came to repudiate the lingering aestheticism which had governed his fascination with the stylized forms of Noh—after all, by 1918 he was dismissing his versions as "too damn soft", and his subsequent mentions of Noh tended to emphasize the "Homeric robustness" of the originals.[22] It's important, though, to see that the effect of his association of temporal discontinuity with forms of artifice was something which would have long-term effects. In other words, we have to be cautious in speaking of Pound's break with "aestheticism," for a certain conception of art as a defence against nature runs through his work and alongside the more widely commented upon celebrations of the natural order.

This is particularly problematic in the case of *Hugh Selwyn Mauberley* where the relation between time, desire and artifice has led to one common misreading of the poem as simply Pound's satirical attack on Mauberley-as-aesthete. Interestingly, though, there has been a recent tendency to emphasize Pound's links to Mauberley, and to see his imaginary character's dilemma as very much his own. I am thinking particularly of an interesting essay by Ronald Bush, which appeared in *American Literary History* in Summer 1990.[23] The opening stage of Bush's argument effectively disposes of the view of *Mauberley* as straightforward satire, even though that was the way Pound himself in later years insisted that it be read. Having put that case, however, Bush's argument seems to me to return to familiar ground, claiming that the second main section of the poem, "Mauberley (1920)," is narrated "with fury" as Pound launches a lacerating critique of a desiccated and sterile poetics which he himself had already renounced and moved beyond. "Medallion" is firmly associated, in Bush's words, "with the irony that saturates the preceding four poems," and the concluding poem presents an evocation of artistic impoverishment, where the woman seems somehow "disfigured and debased," representing "the absence of that which had once made life worth living" (p.68).

And so, to Mauberley, the soprano brings not rebirth through passion but yet another opportunity to compose yet another "face-oval" within yet another (note the grating, period cliché) "suave" bounding line. And are we to feel pity or horror or terror as, "Beneath half-watt rays" that aestheticize the singer no less than the glaze of porcelain, "The eyes turn topaz"? Poor lonely man, who, like Joyce's Gabriel Conroy, would turn his love into a composition

("Distant Music") from the nineties. Ghastly fate, the woman's, whose quick eyes turn in his gaze to stone. (p.72)

Bush passes over the now customary identification of the soprano as Raymonde Collignon, a clue first picked up by Jo Brantley Berryman[24] and subsequently confirmed by the publication of a letter from Pound to Eva Hesse in which he remarks of "Medallion": "Luini: Raymonde Collignon, diseuse, very Luini, type not prevalent in Britain."[25] The poem, Pound continues, entails "merely the contrapunto. or if yu like the clavicord purity of R/s voice vs/ the PYgoddamano, inf/ cx/ of clumsy instrument vs/ the finer . . .Luini/ VURRY definite case of eye-lid and cheek bone." Pound's comment makes it rather difficult to find in the poem the particular emotional registers ("pity or horror or terror") referred to by Bush, whose reading is not in fact clinched at all by "the grating, period cliché 'suave' " which probably alludes to Reinach's account of the head of Aphrodite whose braids are admired in "Medallion" (Reinach writes of an "exquisite suavity of expression"[26]). Add to this Pound's laudatory reference elsewhere to the "thick, suave colour, firm, even" of Rimbaud's "Venus Anadyomène,[27] and the recurring use of the word in visionary contexts in *The Cantos* (from "the suavity of the rock" in *Canto XVII* to the "suave eyes, quiet, not scornful" of *Canto LXXIV*[28]) and Bush's reading seems rather less convincing.

Now we know that Pound had already exhorted himself to "Give up th'intaglio method" in the first of the Ur-Cantos,[29] but his reviews of Collignon's performances strongly suggest that this injunction needs to be read in terms of his own narrative ambitions for an epic poem rather than as an unqualified rejection of the sort of minimalist precisions associated with the soprano's art and his own imagist poems. The "intaglio method" still had its virtues, and if Collignon's art reveals certain limits, it nonetheless shares the spirit of modernism in its rejection of the mimetic. This is just the point Pound makes in a review of one of her performances:

> No one has a more keen perception than she has of the difference between art and life; of the necessary scale and proportion required in the presentation of a thing which is not the photograph and wax-cast, but *a re-creation in different and proportional medium*. As long as this diseuse was on stage she was non-human; she was, if you like, a china image; there are Ming porcelains which are respectable; the term "china" is not in this connection ridiculous.[30]

The reference to recreation in a different medium seems to encapsulate the aim of "Medallion," the perfection of this voice exemplifying the very process by which art transcends both reality and realism (the "wax-cast" recalling *Mauberley*'s "mould in plaster").

Transcendence of a natural order is especially important in *Mauberley*, because it stresses the turn to artifice which Pound's imaginary character seems unable to make. He is himself an anachronism, but cannot (in contrast to his creator) take an active stance toward the past, making anachrony the condition of his own art. He is, much like the Pound of the early poems, *possessed* by the past rather than a re-creator of it ("lacking the skill to forge Achaia"). Part II of the sequence attributes this failure to the disorientation produced in Mauberley by the force of sexual desire. In fact, throughout the poem Pound seems to be connecting a sense of personal anachronism, postponement and even artistic failure with sexual temptation. The landscape of Circe's coral isle "Burst in upon the porcelain revery:/ Impetuous troubling/ Of his imagery", and the power of desire temporarily frustrates the objectivising tendencies Pound associates with authentic avant-garde art. There is a sort of interiorisation of the aesthetic here, with Homer's "ear for the sea-surge" (*Canto VII*) yielding only "the *imaginary*/Audition of the phantasmal sea-surge").[31]

But we still have to reckon with Mauberley's " 'fundamental passion',/ This urge to convey the relation/ Of eye-lid and cheek-bone/ By verbal manifestation." Can we really believe that this is meant to signify a degraded aestheticism? After all, Pound uses the phrase "verbal manifestation" in a variety of strongly affirmative contexts elsewhere,[32] and much later, in *Canto LXXIV*/446, he will recall " . . . cheek bone, by verbal manifestation,/her eyes as in 'La Nascita.' " These seductive and desirous eyes promise pleasure but, as I have said, at the price of a loss of artistic direction and purpose. If we are to fault Mauberley it is surely not for his commitment to linguistic precision but because he "drifts" hedonistically, allowing himself to be possessed by the object of his desire and thus *relaxing* the discipline of "verbal manifestation."

Pound's comments about art as "an armour/Against utter consternation" thus have to be taken quite seriously. If the force of a natural desire threatens to lure the poet (like Odysseus) off course, the only artistic solution to the problem is, Pound seems to suggest, to block any process of narcissistic identification by making the object of desire as "objective" as possible. Clearly, then, the poem proposes an important distinction between the interior world of Mauberley's floating sexual fantasies ("the imaginary /Audition of the phantasmal sea-surge") and the focussed aesthetic perception of the soprano in "Medallion" where Collignon's art is celebrated for being itself "a re-creation in different and proportional medium." Whether we like it or not (and most critics have not), Pound does seem to want the sequence to finish on a high note, with the confusing immediacy of the passion which sets Mauberley drifting finally overcome by making the experience of desire one which is thoroughly *mediated* by previous cultural contexts. In "Medallion," the woman becomes an object of desire only in so far as she is cast in a "different medium" and thereby rendered "non-human" and thoroughly aesthetic.[33] Desire is controlled through a calculated displacement of its object into discontinuous planes and times; the natural is thus transformed to artifice, as the sculptural image of the woman translates time into space, with the anachronous play of allusion, from Luini to King Minos, embodied in the interrelation of surfaces and planes (''metal, or intractable amber''). In repudiating any confusion of the ''caressable'' with artistic values, Pound here deviates quite deliberately from the usual idiom of passionate celebration—it is, for example, *the*, not her, ''sleek head'' which emerges from the frock, and in the typescript he had originally used the very un-erotic ''pate'' instead of ''head.''[34]

''Medallion's'' distanced perception and its rigorously objectified presentation of the singer point, then, not backwards, to a diminished art, but forward, to the intensely stylised visionary and erotic landscapes of *The Cantos*. There as here art offers the necessary supplement to nature, and only in the more clearly contemplative reaches of the late *Cantos* will Pound dream of a nature unalloyed by art, of a nature whose continuous rhythms promise peace and (we might say) trance. Elsewhere, it is time as the time of writing which provides the poem's main discipline and practice, a condition which breaches time's natural flow and makes discontinuity a privileged means of knowledge.

NOTES

1. "From the History of an Infantile Neurosis", *The Pelican Freud Library*, Vol. 9 (Harmondsworth: Penguin Books, 1979), p. 284.

2. *Collected Early Poems of Ezra Pound*, ed. Michael John King (London: Faber and Faber, 1977), p.115. The phrase recalls Yeats's early preference for both remoteness and abstraction, as in his talk of "images that remind us of vast passions, the vagueness of past times, all the chimeras that haunt the edge of trance" (*Essays and Introductions* [New York: Macmillan, 1961), p.243).

3. "Piere Vidal Old", *Ibid.*, p. 109.

4. "Und Drang", *Ibid.*, p. 169.

5. "Histrion", *Ibid.*, p. 71.

6. *Critical Writings of Ford Madox Ford*, ed. Frank MacShane (Lincoln, NB: University of Nebraska Press, 1964), p. 40. Ford goes on to say that impressionism allows for "superimposed emotions", but it is clear from the thrust of his argument that he is concerned primarily with "the record of the impression of a moment", "the impression, not the corrected chronicle" (p. 41).

7. "Vorticism" (1914), in Harriet Zinnes, ed., *Ezra Pound and the Visual Arts* (New York: New Directions, 1980), p. 209.

8. Ibid.

9. Kunio Komparu, *The Noh Theater: Principles and Perspectives* (New York, Tokyo, Kyoto: Weatherhill/Tankosha, 1983), P. 41.

10. Ibid., p. 42.

11. Komparu, *The Noh Theatre*, pp.74–5. Nine of the plays are of this type: *Kayoi Komachi, Kumasaka, Tamura, Tsunemasa, Nishikigi, Awoi No Uye, Chorio, Genjo*, and *Suma Genji*.

12. Nobuko Tsukui, *Ezra Pound and Noh Plays* (Washington, DC.: University Press of America, 1983), p. 3.

13. Komparu, *The Noh Theater*, pp. 87–88.

14. Ibid., p. 77 (my emphases). Cf. Yeats, "Anima Mundi" (1917), *Mythologies* (London: Macmillan, 1962), pp. 355–56: "The dead, as the passionate necessity wears out, come into a measure of freedom and may turn the impulse of events, started while living, in some new direction, but they cannot originate except through the living. Then gradually they perceive, although they are still but living in their memories, harmonies, symbols, and patterns, *as though all were being refashioned by an artist . . .* "

15. Komparu, *The Noh Theater*, p. 86.

16. For a discussion of Pound's own attempt at writing plays modelled on Noh, see my "An Experiment with Time: Ezra Pound and the Example of Japanese Noh," *Modern Language Review*, 90, 1 (January 1995), pp. 1–13.

17. *Nishikigi* was also one of the most important plays for Yeats; see, for example, David Clark, *"Nishikigi* and Yeats's *The Dreaming of the Bones"*, *Modern Drama*, 7 (May 1964), pp. 111–25.

18. This would seem to be the implication of the lines from *Nishikigi* quoted above ("You do not dip twice into the same river").

19. The concept of the "supplement" is used in Derrida's sense of a "necessary surplus"; see *Writing and Difference*, trans. Alan Bass (London: Routledge & Kegan Paul, 1978), pp.211–12.

20. John Forrester, *The Seductions of Psychoanalysis: Freud, Lacan, and Derrida* (Cambridge: Cambridge University Press, 1990), p. 206.

21. "Ideally", because the relative autonomy of different materials was undermined as Pound's project assumed an increasingly ideological cast during and after the thirties. See my "Lost object(s): Ezra Pound and the Idea of Italy", in Richard Taylor and Claus Melchior, eds., *Ezra Pound and Europe* (Amsterdam: Radopi, 1993) for a view of this identification with fascist authority as a form of primary narcissism which prevented the tropic displacement of mourning.

22. *The Selected Letters of Ezra Pound*, ed. D. D. Paige (London: Faber and Faber, 1971), p.137; *Guide to Kulchur* (London: Peter Owen, 1938), p. 81.

23. Ronald Bush, " 'It Draws One to Consider Time Wasted': *Hugh Selwyn Mauberley*", *American Literary History*, 2. 2 (Summer 1990), pp. 56–78. Further references will be given in the text.

24. Jo Brantley Berryman, "Medallion: Pound's Poem", *Paideuma*, 2. 3 (Winter 1973), pp. 391–98.

25. Eva Hesse, "Raymonde Collignon, or (Apropos *Paideuma*, 7–1 & 2, pp. 345–6): The Duck That Got Away," *Paideuma*, 10,3 (Winter 1981), p. 584. While Bush ignores the presence of Collignon in "Medallion" he does observe (p.68) that "the poem presents the persistent suggestion of a figure, at once muse and emotional self, a figure who, whole, would be a woman, eyes shining with vision, mouth informed with song. But with one exception ["Envoi"], this figure is never whole." See my "A Consciousness Disjunct: Sex and the Writer in Ezra Pound's *Hugh Selwyn Mauberley*," *Journal of American Studies*, 28, 1 (April 1994), pp. 61–76, for a more detailed presentation of Collignon's role in the poem.

26. Salomon Reinach, *Apollo: Histoire Générale des Arts Plastiques Professée à L'École du Louvre* (1904; Paris: Librairie Hachette, 1930), p. 58 (figure on 59).

27. "French Poets", in *Make It New* (London: Faber & Faber, 1934), p. 182; noted in Peter Brooker, *A Student's Guide to the Selected Poems of Ezra Pound* (London: Faber & Faber, 1979), p. 224.

28. *The Cantos of Ezra Pound* (London: Faber & Faber, 1975), pp.77, 425 (further references will be given in the text in the form: XVII/77.

29. "Three Cantos. I", *Poetry*, X, 3 (June 1917), p. 113.

30. "Music. By William Atheling", *New Age*, XXVI, 24 (15 April 1920), rpt. in R. Murray Schafer, ed., *Ezra Pound and Music: the Complete Criticism* (London: Faber and Faber, 1978), p. 225.

31. Ian F. A. Bell, "The Phantasmagoria of *Hugh Selwyn Mauberley*," *Paideuma*, V, 3 (Winter 1976), p. 379 observes that Pound's version of the Homeric phrase here "seems deliberately impoverished, suggesting merely the trap of auditory illusion, counterpointing the Sirens' song, 'Caught in the unstopped ear', which traps E.P. in the opening 'Ode pour L'Election de son Sepulchre.' "

32. See, for example, uses of the phrase in *Literary Essays of Ezra Pound*, ed. T. S. Eliot (London: Faber & Faber, 1968), pp. 25, 153.

33. Ian F. A. Bell, "A Mere Surface: Wyndham Lewis, Henry James and the 'Latitude' of *Hugh Selwyn Mauberley*", *Paideuma*, XV, 2–3 (Fall & Winter 1986), p. 58, rightly insists on the difference in this aesthetic between "unhuman" and "inhuman".

34. Typescript of *Mauberley*, reproduced in Jo Brantley Berryman, *Circe's Craft: Pound's Hugh Selwyn Mauberley* (Ann Arbor, MI.: UMI Research Press, 1983), p. 238.

10

RICHARD CADDEL
Secretaries of Nature:
Towards a Theory of Modernist Ecology

Observe the phenomena of nature as one in whom the ancestral
voices speak.

(Analects VI, 11)

I suppose St Hilary looked at an oak-leaf.

(Canto XCV, 647)

I suppose that looking at an oakleaf must be generally accepted to be an act which will heighten one's understanding of the form and function of that natural object, and thus, perhaps, of the economy of such forms. From that, my own predilections lead me to think that nothing is so important for the survival of the planet as that heightening of our understanding of natural economy and ecology—I won't, at this stage, burden you with the specifics of this point, but I will, later, if pressed. You've been warned. It's a polemic I'm prepared to push. Now, I'm still unclear about how far you can make good poetry by pushing polemics—Basil Bunting quite squarely asserts that you don't; Pound, on the other hand, lived and wrote entirely upon the premise that you can and do. What I want to do on this occasion is to take an earlier model of "nature poetry", and then with that, explore some elements of the poetries of Pound and his contemporaries, and see how, directly or indirectly, these all contribute to our ecological perceptions.

This is therefore an exploratory essay, in that it lacks any ready made all-embracing dogma to bring it to a conclusion. It is open-ended: interactive, as opposed to monologic; it's a dynamic system, as opposed to a closed system. In these respects it is both modernist, and ecologist: but—that's not the whole story. It's an address to the act of writing about nature, for an age when nature can no longer be seen as infinite and eternal, and for an age when we can no longer afford to think of nature without thinking of ecology—that is, the science of the complex interrelations of living things. Ezra Pound is late entering my account of all this, but he's going to be involved whenever we try to make the jump from nature poetry to ecological poetry.

Nature poetry has always been about away. There are a few important exceptions to this, one of which I'll mention, but basically, there's a presumption that when you're talking about birds, flowers, trees, mountains etc., there's a human framework, and a natural framework, and that they are two separate things, even when you pop your humans against a natural backdrop. For a long while there was even an assumption that "where man is not, nature is barren"—an attitude which is so far from the literal truth today that we may find it hard to live with. This duality is at the root of much that is problematic in our literary considerations of ecology.

I was therefore initially pleased to come across Jonathan Bate's *Romantic Ecology: Wordsworth and the Environmental Tradition*[1] as a pioneering approach to its subject, an attempt to bridge from perceptions of earlier centuries to our own. Bate's aim is to rescue the grand old poet of nature from the recent welter of socialist criticism by rereading his "green" credentials:

> A green reading of Wordsworth . . . has strong historical force, for if one historicizes the idea of an ecological viewpoint—a respect for the earth and a scepticism as to the orthodoxy that economic growth and material production are the be-all and end-all of human society—one finds oneself squarely in the Romantic tradition; and it has strong contemporary force in that it brings Romanticism to bear on what are likely to be some of the most pressing political issues of the coming decade: the greenhouse effect and the depletion of the ozone layer, the destruction of the tropical rainforest, acid rain, the pollution of the sea, and, more locally, the concreting of England's green and pleasant land.[2]

"Respect" is in fact a weak word for Wordsworth's self- evident reverence for the earth and nature in general, and his chosen local landscape in particular: Bate quotes the following passage from *The Excursion* in his chapter on "The Moral of Landscape":

> O then what soul was his, when, on the tops
> Of the high mountains, he beheld the sun
> Rise up, and bathe the world in light! He looked—
> Ocean and earth, the solid frame of earth
> And ocean's liquid mass, beneath him lay
> In gladness and deep joy. The clouds were touch'd
> And in their silent faces could he read
> Unutterable love. Sound needed none,
> Nor any voice of joy; his spirit drank
> The spectacle; sensation, soul, and form,
> All melted into him; they swallowed up

His animal being; in them did he live,
And by them did he live; they were his life.

Bate describes this passage as "a summation of the Wordsworthian "philoso-phy" of the "one life" and the "active universe"—the theory that there is animation in and unity between all things, and that nature is accordingly entitled to moral consideration."[3]

I'm afraid I can only go a certain way with this. It's a truism that Words-worth loved nature, and achieved his own personal level of union with nature, and that his work testifies to this, very movingly, on numerous occasions. It's true too that he urged others to do so ("Accuse me not / Of arrogance" pleads his Wanderer alter-ego, as he winds up for a particularly didactic bit on the subject). But I'm doubtful about those clouds with faces, and that happy sea: these surely are straightforward examples of the Pathetic Fallacy, and after all, where's Ruskin when you really need him? It seems to me that in order to achieve his spectator's union with nature, Wordsworth's had to, literally, Romanticise it. Then again, there's something almost predatory, or even voyeuristic, I feel, in "his spirit drank / The spectacle": time and again in Wordsworth the meaning, the little slug of doctrine, comes from watching something, being a spectator to nature, rather than actually being part of it. I don't feel that the "unity between all things" has been amply demonstrated here. The message seems to be still that nature is something you go to, you drink from, and you come away refreshed. The "moral consideration" to which nature is entitled still seems to be of a very restricted kind.

How often one finds that the Romantic sensitivity to natural things is related, at its root, to a kind of tourism, a relief from the "overflowing streets" —as if the turbulence of the industrial revolution city had actually created the need for the perceived timelessness of the natural landscape. The dualism I've referred to becomes explicit at this stage—man in one place, nature in another, except during stimulating peregrinations; man bustling; nature constant. Bate doesn't quote the bit where young Wordsworth acknowledges a timelessness in nature:

> A Child, I held unconscious intercourse
> With the eternal Beauty, drinking in
> A pure organic pleasure from the lines
> Of curling mist, or from the level plain
> Of waters colour'd by the steady clouds.[4]

Note that we're still "drinking" here. That was the 1805 version of "The Prelude..In the 1850 version "eternal" becomes "Old as creation"—the feel-ing's very much the same, but does perhaps reflect a shift of consciousness.

The Romantic exception is John Clare, the "peasant poet" of Helpston, to whom Bate affords little more than a passing reference. Clare, according to Bate, endorses this view of "The Eternity of Nature":

> The daisy lives and strikes its little root
> Into the lap of time—centurys may come
> And pass away into the silent tomb . . .
> Aye still the child with pleasure in his eye
> Shall cry "The daisy"—a familiar cry—
> And run to pluck it.[5]

Bate doesn't point out that here, as on countless other occasions, Clare's human is a destroyer, undermining the outward meaning of the text. It fell to Clare, ultimately, to see that the natural world around him was not eternal, as woods and hedgerows were grubbed up for land enclosures, birds and animals hunted to extinction for sport, the great wetlands of Wisbech Fen drained and so on. When Clare wrote of birds, animals, trees and so forth he did it on the basis of what he'd lived with, and recorded, with something akin to desperation. But you could give an amateur naturalist his description of a nightingale, and he'd know where to look for it, and when he'd found it, and how it behaved. The same is not true of other Romantic poets: Wendell Berry flatly asserts that "though Wordsworth was preoccupied with the experience of nature, there is remarkably little in the way of particular observation to be found in him."[6] Clare's business, founded on direct knowledge and observation, was to attempt to create his paradise of the mind directly from the materials of his world. He became the chronicler, the observer, of the natural and social ecology in which he lived, and which was disintegrating around him. Clare, of course, went mad.

This definition of nature as the timeless restorer is in perfect accord with contemporary Conservative political thought, which seeks to limit nature to specified nature reserves, cared for within the tourist amenity framework. Wordsworth himself had some inkling of this tendency towards the end of his life, as he watched the destructive march—or rail route—of commercial tourism into his own beloved landscape—a landscape popularized to a great extent, ironically, by his own "Guide to the Lakes," a book so popular that Matthew Arnold could recall meeting a cleric who asked if the author had written anything else. What thou lovest well, in fact, becomes highly vulnerable. Perhaps this is why the word "eternal" in the passage I've quoted had to be modified. And once you can accept a nature which is eternal and somewhere else you can probably accept the idea of a place to put waste which is forever somewhere else (though you probably won't want to write poems about that). That's not the ecological framework I'm looking for.

I want an ecology which is based on real observation, as opposed to spectator status, and which allows no separation between the "human" and "natural" world, and no concept of eternity. This announces formally the death of "nature poetry" as a distinct branch, forgive me, of the art. I'm looking to the poets and poetics of Modernism to offer me a more flexible, dynamic model.

Pound staked out a theoretical position on the man-nature proximity equation as early as 1910, and showed no signs of moving away from it at any stage in his career:

> Our kinship to the ox we have constantly thrust upon
> us; but beneath this is our kinship to the vital universe, to the
> tree and the living rock, and, because this is less obvious—and
> possibly more interesting—we forget it.[7]

Kinship is an interesting word, and Guy Davenport[8] has already pointed to early Pound poems (such as "The Tree") and found a closeness of association which is telling:

> I stood still and was a tree amid the wood,
> Knowing the truth of things unseen before . . . ("The Tree")

Davenport adds, "That a tree can be a persona at all is startling [. . .] Trees are everywhere in Pound's poetry, and become symbols of extraordinary power and beauty in *Rock-Drill*, *Thrones*, and the cantos now in draft form for the poem's conclusion."

I don't think I'm ready, on the strength of this, to describe Ezra Pound as the voice of ecological poetry. What I'd like to do instead is pick out some groups of the natural images which occur, particularly in the late *Cantos*, and try to draw them together into some sort of pattern. There's a lot to cover, so I'll say here and now that I don't claim to be comprehensive.

Pound consistently urged close observation: *ABC of Reading* opens with the story of naturalist Louis Agassiz forcing his postgraduate student to write directly about a decaying fish, and leads directly to:

> 1 Let the pupil write the description of a tree.
> 2 Of a tree without mentioning the name of the tree (larch,
> pine, etc.) so that the reader will not mistake it for the descrip-
> tion of some other kind of tree.[9]

It needs to be stressed that this kind of detailed seeing—the close experiential observation of an Agassiz—is worlds apart from the "beholding" of Wordsworth, wherein the I-thou relationship is maintained steadfastly intact. I hope I shall make it plain that for me it's at the heart of any construction of modernist ecology.

I'm going to begin with the *Pisan Cantos*. I've always loved the musical algebra of those birds, coming and going on the wire of the DTC throughout Canto 79 (p485–):

> with 8 birds on a wire
> or rather on 3 wires [. . .]
> 4 birds on 3 wires, one bird on one [. . .]
> 5 of 'em now on 2;
> on 3; 7 on 4
> thus what's his name
> and the change in writing the song books
> 5 on 3 [. . .]
>   2 on 2 . . .
> 3 on 3 . . .
> with 6 on 3, swallow-tails . . .

—and so on. And then the birds in *Canto 82*, 525:

> Till the cricket hops
>   but does not chirrp in the drill field
> 8th day of September
>   f
>   d
>   g
>   write the birds in their treble scale
> Terreus! Terreus!

There's a bit of myth here and there, and I have to say that I won't be dealing with myth in this article. Note how Pound's ideogramatic method enables him to place his materials close together into little language groups, or, if you like, ecosystems. Basically, we're being made to look at and listen to real birds—as Pound had so much occasion to do at this stage—in their surroundings. Throughout these *Cantos* there is observed nature in one form or another: clouds, light, insects, grass, plants, and so on. We can even note the natural climate:

> If the hoar frost grip thy tent
> Thou wilt give thanks when night is spent.

(*Canto 84*, 540)

That's a measure of directness, of experiential closeness to things. And around these images, the full panoply of Poundian argument goes on, seemingly unabated: tax systems, bits of Confucius, fragments of a paradise. The argument is not unrelated to the observed; thus:

> and there was a smell of mint under the tent flaps
> especially after the rain

> (*Canto 74*, 428)

These lines are linked to the "mint, thyme and basilicum" of *Canto 79*, 487), and other places where such herbs are cited as paradisal signifiers.

Perhaps the most famous sequence is the birth of the wasp in *Canto 83*, 520:

> and Brother Wasp is building a very neat house
> of four rooms, one shaped like a squat indian bottle
> La vespa, la vespa, mud, swallow system . . .
> and in the warmth after chill sunrise
> an infant, green as new grass,
> has stuck its head or tip
> out of Madame La Vespa's bottle

> mint springs up again
>   in spite of Jones' rodents
> as had the clover by the gorilla cage
>   with a four-leaf

> When the mind swings by a grass-blade
>   an ant's forefoot shall save you
> the clover leaf smells and tastes as its flower
>   The infant has descended,
>   from mud on the tent roof to Tellus,
> like to like colour he goes amid grass-blades

Gilbert White and David Attenborough could hardly do the descriptive bit better. Note the Franciscan echo—"Brother Wasp"— linking again to the kinship bit.

We should briefly try to sum up what sort of nature we're being presented with here:

—It's the only kind of nature Pound had around him at the time: the whole of the *Pisan Cantos* is written with a very apparent restricted reference set—few books, brilliant fragments from an extraordinary memory, snatches of conversation and DTC daily life, and these directly observed bits of "natural world".

    —It's immediate, close at hand, appealing directly to physical perception (no duality here), and it presents an open ecosystem wherein a range of phenomena—from DTC guards to paradisal herbs—can interact.

    —It's fragmentary, ever-changing, fragile, dynamic, and a whole lot of other things which add up to NON-ETERNAL.

    When you put that lot together, it seems to me that you make a significant breakthrough in ecological perception.

    As the over-riding rationale for these (and other) passages from the *Pisan Cantos*, we are offered statements of a more doctrinal nature: such as, from the much quoted "vanity" canto (*Canto 81*, 521):

> The ant's a centaur in his dragon world.
> Pull down thy vanity, it is not man
> Made courage, or made order, or made grace,
>   Pull down thy vanity, I say pull down.
> Learn of the green world what can be thy place
>   In scaled invention or true artistry.

Wendell Berry asserts that these "lines could serve as the epigraph of the science of ecology."[10] In the context of the *Pisan Cantos* they represent a dialectic which has been earned by direct experience.

    Moving on, predictably enough, to the John Heydon passages from *Rock Drill*: other commentators (Baumann,[11] Surette,[12] etc.) have described Pound's association with this alchemist-cum-natural scientist-cum-astrologer of the seventeenth century. He described himself (as Pound quotes) as "Secretary of Nature" on the title page of his *Holy Guide* (1662). It's worth being clear that "secretary" here means, not one who takes notes, etc., but simply a repository, a storer of wisdom and so forth. It's a boast, in fact. Setting aside the early "Ur-Canto" references to Heydon's vision of a kind of green goddess (Heydon at this stage is "half-cracked" by Pound's own estimation), we come upon him in *Rock Drill* associated with the neo-platonic material, and with Apollonius, and with Mencius:

>   "We have", said Mencius, "but phenomena."
> monumenta. In nature are signatures
>   needing no verbal tradition,
> oak leaf never plane leaf. John Heydon.

>   (*Canto 87*, 573)

that is, you must observe the oak leaf; know its difference in form and function from other leaves. Be that close.

The doctrine of signatures (not Heydon's but one which Heydon unashamedly pinched when it suited him) is a well-documented one. It comes down from Paracelsus via Giambattista Porta, and had already been denounced by field naturalists two generations before Heydon. By Porta's stating of it, God has placed a sign or hint on various natural products (mostly plants) to indicate their potential medicinal uses—"whereas if a man be ignorant hereof, he loseth the greatest part of the knowledge of secret operation and works of nature."[13] One can see why signatures—a kind of natural equivalent of ideograms—would appeal to Pound, if not in their own right, then as models for tracing affinities. But they're fraught with problems, and many of them come from writers who, like John Heydon, simply regurgitated the guff they'd had handed down to them by earlier writers, paraphrasing a bit here and there. Thus, to take an example of Heydon's signatures quoted by Pound, with a Dante preface:

> And from this Mount were blown
> seed
> and that every plant have its seed
> so will the weasel eat rue,
> and the swallows nip celandine

> (*Canto 92*, 618)

What Heydon actually says (in his *Holy Guide*, which Pound had by him in St. Elizabeths, borrowed from Mrs. Yeats) is, "The Weasel, when she is to encounter the Serpent, arms herself with eating of Rue."—and "The Swallows make use of Celandine." Both stories are lifted from Gerard, probably the Johnson edition of 1633—or else from a source so similar it can only be an intermediary, thus: "it is reported, That . . . when the Weesel is to fight with the Serpent she armeth herself by eating rue against the might of the Serpent" and "Some hold the opinion that with this herbe the dammes restore sight to their young ones when their eies be out: the which things are vaine and false."[14] We could go on to demonstrate where the idea of calling Greater Celandine "Swallow-wort" comes from, or just what Dioscorides says about the properties of rue, or what modern animal dietary studies and field naturalists have to say about the likelihood of swallows and weasels eating herbs anyway. And we can note the inspired way Pound animates the phrase by altering "make use of" to "nip": "the swallows nip celandine." But, folks, we can save time looking out for its actually happening: it doesn't in either case, and it didn't when either Pound or Heydon were around to look for it, which I bet they didn't. We're a long way from the precisions of Louis Agassiz making his pupils experience the truth of what they wrote, or St. Hilary looking at an oak leaf in order to appreciate its true nature, or the emphasis which Pound repeatedly placed upon observation.

Should it matter to me if Pound recycles some duff information for us? We don't try to take the Dante bit in the preceding lines as a literal statement on seed dispersal, just as we don't try to take the griffins digging up gold (*Canto 94*, 637) as anything other than an image from Apollonius. Heaven knows it's not the only occasion on which Pound offers us some fairly dubious matter for his own purposes; usually we take it in the spirit it's offered. Well, it matters enough for me to point it out as incorrect: swallows and weasels are close enough to our kin, within the life-frame model which Pound had established in Pisa, at great personal cost, for us to worry about such things, especially if we're given a context of Pound's insistence upon observation, of "We have," said Mencius, "but phenomena." It's not good enough to repeat someone else's unverified (and unverifiable) data thus.

Well, after all, we're able "To confess wrong without losing rightness" (*Canto 116*, 797): as the *Cantos* progress into the Joseph Rock material in "Thrones" we're on surer ground among the close observations of a field scientist. The point here, the reason why Rock's work meant so much to Pound, is suggested by Peter Makin[15]: "the literature shows that the entities of the landscape have penetrated every element of the¹Na-²khi imaginative life, as (in the¹Na-²khi eyes) beauty." So that there's no gap between their lives, their rites, and their environment. The trees, as Davenport noted, are everywhere: "The hills here are blue-green with juniper" and the bears eat acorns. Here Pound lets in another character, Elzeard Bouffier:

> Bouffier,
> Elzeard has made the forest at Vergons
> under Kuanon's eye there is oak-wood
> (*Canto 101*, 725)

Thus, by the perception and action of a Provençal farmer, we can equate bits of Europe with Rock's lost paradise. The image of the tree-planter, by the way, cropped up earlier in *Canto 87*, 573, shortly after the Mencius/John Heydon bit: "Baccin said: I planted that / tree, and that tree (ulivi)." I leave that around, for what it's worth. The idea of a science of natural order is asserted over and over again. Here is a part of *Canto 99*, 711:

> But the four TUAN
> are from nature
> jen, i, li, chih

Not from the descriptions in the school house;

—here we're closer again to the spirits both of Agassiz, and of "Learn of the green world."

I can't resist one last bit of observational, experiential material, from the fragment of *Canto 115*, 794, where this particular Pound reader started, in 1968:

> Night under wind mid garofani
>   the petals are almost still
> Mozart, Linnaeus, Sulmona,
> When one's friends hate each other
>   how can there be peace in the world?
> Their asperities diverted me in my green time.
> A blown husk that is finished
>   but the light sings eternal
> a pale flare over marshes
>   where the salt hay whispers to tide's change

Makin says that critics have simply quoted those last lines and forgotten to write criticism. I'm going to uphold that tradition. And yet, I remain totally enchanted by it.

NOTES

1. Jonathan Bate. *Romantic Ecology: Wordsworth and the Environmental Tradition*. London: Routledge, 1991.

2. Bate p. 9.

3. Bate p. 66.

4. William Wordsworth. *The Prelude, or the Growth of a Poet's Mind*. Ed. Ernest de Selincourt. London: OUP, 1933.

5. Bate p. 54.

6. Wendell Berry. "A Secular Pilgrimage." *Hudson Review* 23 (1970): 401–24.

7. Ezra Pound. *The Spirit of Romance*. Norfolk, Conn.: New Directions, 1959.

8. Guy Davenport. "Persephone's Ezra." *New Approaches to Ezra Pound*. Ed. Eva Hesse. London: Faber, 1969. 145–73.

9. Ezra Pound. *ABC of Reading*. London: Faber, 1951.

10. Berry p. 415.

11. Baumann, Walter. "Secretary of Nature, J. Heydon." Hesse 303–18.'

12. Surette, Leon. *A Light from Eleusis: A Study of Ezra Pound's Cantos*. Oxford: Clarendon, 1979.

13. (herbals)

14. Gerard, John. *The Herball, or Generall Historie of Plantes*. Ed. Thomas Johnson. London, 1633.

15. Makin, Peter. *Pound's Cantos*. London: Allen & Unwin, 1985.

CONTRIBUTORS

1. *Massimo Bacigalupo* is Professor of American Literature at the University of Genoa, Italy.

2. *Richard Caddel* is Director of the Basil Bunting Poetry Centre at the University of Durham, England.

3. *Anne Conover Carson* lives in Washington, D.C, and is the author of *Olga Rudge & Ezra Pound*.

4. *Michael Faherty* is Senior Lecturer in English Literature at De Montfort University, Bedford, England.

5. *Philip Grover* is Senior Lecturer in English (Retired) at the University of Sheffield, England, and now lives in Nontron, France.

6. *Peter Makin* is Professor of English at Kansai University, Japan.

7. *Peter Nicholls* is Professor of English and American Studies at the University of Sussex, England.

8. *Alan Peacock* is Professor of English (Retired) at the University of Ulster at Colerain, Northern Ireland.

9. *Massimo Pesaresi* is Professor of Italian at the Italian Academy for Advanced Studies in America (Columbia University), New York.

10. *William Pratt* is Professor of English Emeritus at Miami University, Oxford, Ohio.

INDEX